Revisiting literacy

Helping readers and writers

JUDITH SMITH AND
ANNE ALCOCK

Open University Press
Milton Keynes · Philadelphia

Open University Press
Celtic Court
22 Ballmoor
Buckingham MK18 1XW

and
1900 Frost Road, Suite 101
Bristol, PA 19007, USA

First Published 1990

British Library Cataloguing in Publication Data

Smith, Judith
    Revisiting literacy: helping readers and writers. -
    (Rethinking reading)
    1. Children. Reading skills. development
    I. Title II. Alcock, Anne III. Series
    428.4'3

    ISBN 0-335-09571-2
    ISBN 0-335-09570-4 (pbk)

Library of Congress Cataloging-in-Publication Data

Smith, Judith, 1933–
    Revisiting literacy : helping readers and writers / Judith Smith
    and Anne Alcock.
        p. cm. -- (Rethinking reading)
    ISBN 0-335-09571-2   ISBN 0-335-09570-4 (pbk.)
    1. Reading (Elementary) 2. Language arts--Remedial teaching.
    3. Literacy. I. Alcock, Anne, 1944- . II. Title. III. Series.
    LB1573.S757   1990
    372.4--dc20   89-39076 CIP

Typeset by Burns & Smith Ltd., Derby
Printed in Great Britain by St Edmundsbury Press,
Bury St Edmunds, Suffolk

Revisiting literacy

RETHINKING READING

Series Editor: L. John Chapman
School of Education, The Open University

Contents

Acknowledgements

Writing this book is our response to the students we have taught over the years. They have been our teachers and we hope that what we have learned will in turn be of help to other teachers and other students.

Without the support and forbearance of our families, and in particular of our husbands, Layton and Tony, this book would never have been written. To them we offer our thanks.

We must also acknowledge the advice and encouragement given to us by our friends and colleagues, Don Burnes and Judy Gray. It has been invaluable.

The authors and publisher are grateful to the following for permission to reproduce copyright material: Thomas Nelson Australia, Melbourne: *Animal Mothers and Babies* (1984), pp. 3 and 15, J. Smith and B. Parkes; *The Hobyahs* (1987), p. 5, B. Parkes and J. Smith; *The Musicians of Bremen* (1987), pp. 2 and 3, B. Parkes and J. Smith. Also Martin Educational, Sydney, Australia: *How to Grow Crystals* (1986), H. Anderson; *The Platypus* (1987), J. Short, J. Green and B. Bird; *Growing Radishes and Carrots* (1986), F. Bolton and D. Snowball.

CHAPTER 1

From theory to practice

Society today demands that people be able to read and write and penalizes those who cannot. Being illiterate usually means being poor and often unemployed or underemployed. Illiteracy means being unable to interact with others through one of the most pervasive media – that of print. Being illiterate excludes people from making use of some of the most important resources of information and enjoyment available. Clearly, schools and teachers are expected to accept responsibility for ensuring that children become literate.

The failure of some children to learn to read and write as soon or as effectively as other children is a matter for concern to those children, their parents and families, their teachers, and to the community in general. These are the people to whom this book is addressed in the hope that it will provide a variety of relevant and enjoyable situations through which children who are not succeeding may be invited to revisit literacy. The suggestions could apply either in the regular classroom or in special intervention settings, with small groups or individual children.

Why some children are slower than others in learning literacy

The search for explanations as to why children fail to become effective readers and writers has gone on for many years. Terms such as specific learning disabilities, specific learning difficulties, and dyslexia have been used in defining and identifying groups of such learners. Tansley and Panckhurst (1981) in their review of theories of why some people fail, suggested that such factors as brain damage, maturational delay, genetic factors, perceptual and motor difficulties, and cognitive difficulties, cause learning problems.

While there is considerable evidence to show that some learners display such problems, no 'cures' yet exist, and these problems must be dealt with in educational settings. Teachers must help such learners through applying what they know about the nature of language itself and about the nature of language learning to help resolve the difficulties displayed by learners. And learners need opportunities to visit and revisit literacy because literacy is learned through use.

Other factors implicated in written language-learning difficulties and delays are social in origin. As Chapman (1987: 10–11) points out:

> because of the level of literacy and values transmitted to them in interaction with their parents, some children slip into the school environment easily and painlessly. In many cases these children come into school already reading and writing...Others, from a teacher's viewpoint are not so fortunate. Their parents' values are different and their concerns are not academic...

As Chapman explains, the causes for the difficulties and delays that children experience in learning to read and write are varied. The language used in the home is a different variety from that of school, so children may not understand the teacher's language. It is becoming widely recognized that much literacy learning is accomplished by some children prior to school as the result of their experiences with reading and writing in their daily lives (Baghban 1984; Harste, Woodward and Burke 1984). Such learning is achieved very informally as children are engaged in situations in which reading and writing is purposeful and relevant to what is happening. Children explore print because it is important and meaningful to them and to those around them, and they learn as they explore. They may, for example, help their parents 'write' shopping lists. They enjoy 'reading' and being read to. They have opportunities to visit literacy as it arises in their lives. These experiences lead to the use of forms of language such as the patterns of language and grammar, and print-format features, appropriate to the situation and the text. Learners therefore have the opportunity to learn the forms of written language as they are involved in exploring the different situations which give rise to the use of such features of language.

Other children do not learn to read and write because of events occurring during their schooling. Here we might include children whose schooling is interrupted by illness or by frequent changes in schools or teachers. Others experience a lack of consistent approaches in what is taught to them about reading and writing. This may leave them confused and unsure about the nature of reading and writing and the strategies that readers and writers use. Again, we would suggest the solution is an educational one, involving the exploration of reading and writing in situations and for purposes which are meaningful to the children.

The nature of language and language learning

We would suggest then that, whatever the reason for the delays and difficulties revealed by their students, teachers must help learners through applying what they know about the nature of language and of language learning to overcoming problems. Teachers can apply their knowledge to the evaluation of their students' performance as language users.

The use of language involves the creation of meaning by speakers and listeners, readers and writers, about experiences they wish to share. Where spoken language is often about what is happening, reading and writing have to rely upon language alone to create meaning. Continuity of meaning is created through relating what readers and writers know from past experience to the situation created through the text. Language is used to link ideas together and so generates cohesion within the text (Chapman 1987).

As teachers of reluctant and inexperienced readers and writers we must be very conscious of their need for prior experiences with similar situations. If necessary we must provide opportunities in our classrooms which will ensure that they have an adequate background knowledge to bring to written text. This, of course, helps them to infer the meanings of words they do not know, and removes some of the emphasis they might otherwise place on word recognition or decoding print.

The structure of situations and language

Every type of socially recognized situation (or genre) has a structure arising from the nature and order of events that normally occur in that type of situation. Experiences of situations provide readers and writers with an awareness of this underlying organization or structure. For example, when we go shopping, we offer to buy the goods and the seller agrees to sell; then we hand over our money to the seller, completing the transaction. From our experiences of reading or having stories read to us we become familiar with the structure of stories. The structure of each situation is reflected in the related text.

Structure varies in different types of situations or genres, and therefore in the related text. The sense of knowing about situations and their text structures is one of the most powerful resources that are available to us as it allows us to respond with confidence to the situation and the language, whether spoken or written. There are also other important relationships between genre and the nature of language that is used. The patterns of language including syntax and grammar vary from situation to situation.

Learning to read and write also involves learning the sound-print or graphophonic relationships. Early researchers in the field of reading difficulties and in particular of dyslexia tended to focus only on this aspect of written language. Today it is recognized that this is only one feature of written language and it must be considered in conjunction with other features identified above.

All aspects of language should be learned within a total context and text. Findings reported by Chapman (1987) demonstrate that poor readers tend to lack awareness of cohesion in text, i.e. they are unaware of the links within text. This interferes with their understanding of what they read. Approaches to helping poor readers and writers should therefore emphasize the situation and the text as a whole. In this way the purposefulness and meaning of the whole provide a lens through which the features of literacy can be investigated.

Why language is learned

People use language to communicate – language, whether it is spoken or written, is essentially a social event. Language too is always an integral part of the situation to which it refers, at least in the mind of the user. Each time people use language, they are involved in a mental trip (Harste and Short 1988) which occurs as they have opportunities to use and reflect upon language in use. They are involved in decisions about the most effective strategies for creating meaning and achieving their purposes.

It is therefore vital that we share the strategies we use to achieve our purposes through language with learners. They in their turn will try out and use the strategies that they see others use successfully in order to achieve their own purposes. And what they learn will be meaningful and relevant to them so they will use these strategies again on other occasions and in similar situations. So that, for instance, we need to make clear to inexperienced readers what strategies we use when we are reading and writing. One of the key features of this book is the consideration of how such strategies can be shared with learners in the varying situations we have outlined.

It is critical therefore that we identify very carefully the social situations that are relevant and important to learners and their culture, as the basis for language learning in the classroom. People learn language and literacy as they are involved in the situations which arise in their lives. They learn the appropriate ways of using language in such situations as they learn about the situations. Language is learned because it is purposeful and meaningful to the learner. The relevance of the situation to the learner is therefore the paramount consideration in planning and teaching inexperienced and reluctant readers and writers.

In this book we are therefore concerned to identify situations and language which will be relevant to slower learners, and so provide fresh opportunities for them to revisit and reflect upon literacy in use.

Teaching approaches for revisiting literacy

Approaches to teaching underachieving readers and writers should be based upon the knowledge that the most vital element is that the learner must be absorbed and engaged in what is going on. The language must be centred in situations that are purposeful and meaningful to the learner.

There are no more powerful models for language teaching than those through which we all learn to speak (Cambourne 1984). The fundamental process used by parents and others involved with young children is the sharing of meaningful language with the children within the situation to which it relates. The situation provides the learner with all types of additional information which supports the learner's efforts to unravel the language. For example, when mother or father and children go shopping, the children see all the goods on display, the written signs around and about, and watch as their parent checks the shopping list and selects the goods, often knowing as well why the goods are needed because of earlier discussion at home.

In the same way, literacy experiences must be related to events and people which learners know and care about. The creation of such situations in the classroom provides the framework for the written language shared with learners. Teachers may, for example, take learners for a literacy walk during which they will identify the types of written language that exist in the neighbourhood and decide the reasons why such language is used. When the children return to the classroom, they can then select examples they would use and explore the uses of such language in more detail. They might notice the signs in shops or the library which inform the public where similar items are stored and decide to make signs to serve the same purpose for classroom equipment. The classroom setting then provides the opportunities for the thinking about and revisiting of language that relate to the original situation.

Or again, if teachers are sharing stories with the children, then they should explore the ideas in the story, through drama, art, writing, story telling and other media so that the story situation comes to life again for the children. The classroom must be a place which invites children to learn because the literacy and the experiences to which the reading and writing relate are important and purposeful to them.

Two questions should therefore be asked in judging the value of the contexts teachers create in their classrooms if they are to be valuable in helping underachieving learners, and indeed all learners, learn about literacy:

• What reasons exist in the situation which would ensure that the learner would want to be involved with the written language either as reader or writer? These reasons may be personal or social. The learner might, for example, be interested in a story or want to find out some specific information, and you as the teacher may help create these purposes for involvement. Or the learner may want to be involved collaboratively with other learners in accomplishing some shared task of reading or writing.
• Would a proficient literacy user be involved in the ways in which learners are involved? If this standard is applied, it means that the literacy tasks proposed will be only those that learners see others accomplishing. If so, literacy learning will be functional.

When such conditions exist, teachers have the opportunity to demonstrate the purposes for which literacy is used and the decisions readers and writers must make. Teachers must also expect learners to succeed, just as parents of young children expect their children will learn to talk – if not immediately, then perhaps the next day, or the following one. Teachers must retain their confidence in the children, even though it is probable that after their previous experiences children may have no confidence in themselves. And this is often the most difficult barrier to overcome.

Learners must be encouraged to read and write for themselves – actually to make the decisions that readers and writers make. It is very easy to take over the job as writer and accept the children's dictation. Yet, when we do so, we are taking away opportunities for them to think about writing. Or, if we only read to them and do not involve them in sharing reading with us, again we are not encouraging them to think and act like readers, needed to ensure they will be successful. The concept of sharing is therefore crucial in the early stages.

Poor readers and writers must also be encouraged to accept responsibility and take risks in making decisions as literacy users. In these circumstances it is vital that teachers accept children's nonconventional responses or approxima-tions. Just as people are accepting when young children use unusual grammar and articulation in their early efforts to speak, so too beginning literacy learners approximate in their efforts to use written language. They will not always read or write in the ways that we expect. But children's approximations provide them with the experience they need. And our concern is that they are gradually becoming closer to our expectations as readers, story tellers, users of grammar, spelling, handwriting, and other aspects of language. Teachers' willingness to accept the less than perfect gives learners in turn the confidence to try again, knowing that their teachers are there to support and help them.

In the following chapters we will outline situations which are responsive to the needs of the very beginning literacy user who needs to awaken to literacy. The process of sharing forms the basis at this first level of learning.

Secondly, we will focus upon literacy experiences in ways which will encourage learners to become more independent as literacy users.

CHAPTER 2

Awakening to literacy

The needs of inexperienced readers and writers

Inexperienced learners need to discover:

- the purposes of reading and writing;
- that written language conveys meaning;
- that written language is coherent and cohesive and relates to coherent and important situations in their lives;
- the strategies that readers and writers use.

We can think of no better way to talk about the needs of inexperienced, or beginning, readers and writers than to consider their needs to become aware of the role of literacy in their lives. Learners must recognize the purposes for which written language is important and useful to them. The ultimate motivation for learning to read and write is the knowledge that reading and writing really can help people achieve their wishes and hopes in various ways and communicate with others.

To help build the bridge between literacy in the classroom and beyond, the meanings in texts must recapture elements of children's lives. They must be able to connect the meanings of what they read and write to things they know. And, as they make these connections, they will also learn new things as a result of reading and writing.

Learners too must come to understand that written language texts are not random, but provide a coherent and meaningful view of the situation which the language they are reading and writing is helping to create. Without this knowledge inexperienced readers and writers, and particularly those who have been unsuccessful over a period of time, approach written texts without any concept of what might occur next. They have no framework from which they can derive meaning. They have no expectations of what might follow.

Coherence in situation is reflected in the language of the text and provides efficient readers and writers with the knowledge that they can predict and confirm what will follow. It allows them to use a variety of cognitive and social strategies to arrive at meaning if there is some aspect of the message of the text they are questioning. Yet so many poor readers and writers appear to look upon written text as isolated from any situation and as consisting of random and unrelated ideas.

Teachers too must demonstrate to their students the mental journeys or strategies that they use as readers and writers as they are involved in reading and writing. And learners, for their part, must learn to use strategies to work out the problems that arise as they read and write.

Observing inexperienced readers and writers

The framework for planning for beginning literacy learners is based on the observation of what they know and what they still need to learn about written language in relation to purpose, meaning and to their use of strategies as readers and writers. Evaluation should always be integrally related to what is happening in the classroom. Our understanding of learners' needs will therefore be gained as we watch them read and write within different situations.

Set out below are several situations through which observations can be made during literacy experiences you might wish to include in your teaching programme.

Observational technique 1

What books do learners enjoy?

It is suggested that these observations can be made as children select books. Discussing books that people have or might read is, after all, something which readers do enjoy.

Resources needed   Have a wide selection of books and other written materials available. These might include:

- a *traditional* story, well illustrated, so that a nonreader can identify the story from the pictures alone;
- a *factual* book, also well illustrated;
- a *cartoon* or *comic* book;
- a *recipe* or other 'how to' (*procedural*) text;
- a *reference* book;
- a book or other text the children are familiar with.

You might also include at least one book with large print and at least one that is mainly print with few illustrations.

The materials are representative of a range of different types of texts and therefore provide a variety of features.

The experience   Invite the child to choose one of the books and discuss why he or she might like to read it, or have it read. As the child selects the book, observe how the book is handled, and the ways in which the content is surveyed:

- Does the child look carefully at the title, and try to read this?
- Ask the child to predict what the book might be about.
- See whether the child looks at any special features such as illustrations or, in the case of a more able reader, at special text features such as a table of contents or chapter headings.
- Discuss the reasons why the child would like or not like to read the resource. The discussion which follows will raise questions such as:
  - the expected content of the text;
  - what type of text it might be, e.g. story, recipe;
  - features about print and illustrations, book length and so on.

You might choose to conclude this experience by having the child draw a character or an episode from a favourite story, or an illustration of a favourite cartoon character. A wall poster of 'Things we read' could be created from different children's responses. These could be captioned to indicate who made the choice and why.

While the book selection outlined above is probably one you would wish to use with inexperienced readers, this observational technique can, and should, be used with readers of a wide variety of achievements. Of course the range of books will vary with the type of evaluation you wish to make. You might use this technique, for example, to observe how effectively learners are using reference materials or their interest in a broad range of literature. The experience itself is a relevant and functional one to all readers: everyone enjoys talking about books.

Observational technique 2

Tell a story

A well-structured story has:

- a setting: telling who, when, where;
- a number of episodes: each involving conflict and resolution which set the stage for what is to follow;
- A finale which concludes the story and resolves the final episode in a quite definite way.

However, this awareness grows with children's involvement with stories. Very young children begin by linking aspects together through association, 'There is a mummy and a daddy. And there is a dog and a cat...', moving to some focus upon a central character and things done by that character. *Rosie's Walk* by Pat Hutchens is a story which has this type of sequence, as Rosie in her walk through the farmyard visits places that are typically found there.

From this step, children usually move from an awareness of action to a sense of the underlying sequence or structure of the story. All of this points to the importance of many experiences with predictable stories. They provide a sequence which is well defined and recurrent before some final dramatic episode, such as the wolf coming down the chimney, leading to a conclusion such as the wolf was never seen again.

Many learners who are delayed in learning to use written language will display delays in their awareness of the structure of stories. This may be due to lack of appropriate experience, or to their inability to capitalize on experience as efficiently as other children. Whatever the case, teachers must share with them insights about stories to provide a foundation for them to enjoy this vital form of literacy.

The following is both an observational technique for evaluating children's sense of learning about stories and also an opportunity for learning.

Resources needed   Your own favourite book and a comprehensive collection of well illustrated stories.

The experience   Select a story which will appeal to your students. Do not read the story but retell it in your own words, sharing the illustrations from the book with your pupils as you do so.

Now invite your learners to select a book and tell you a story. For this shared experience it is important to have a variety of well-illustrated books available. Include some titles you know that may have been read to your children before.

As they tell their stories you will have the opportunity to note various aspects of story knowledge that your children have already acquired. You will be able to observe whether:

- they use a traditional beginning, for example, 'Once upon a time', or a traditional ending, for example, 'the end' or 'was never seen again';
- they have the ability to use words to link the episodes of a story, such as 'then' or 'every day'. You will also be able to observe whether they use words or intonation patterns which show an understanding of the conflicts in stories such as 'suddenly' or 'in a moment';
- their development of a sense of the characters and the dramatic impact of the story. This will be reflected in the language learners use to discuss aspects of stories, such as 'a wicked old giant', 'the mean old Hobyahs';
- consistent use of past tense.

Observational technique 3

A written conversation

Carolyn Burke suggested this experience which is outlined in Goodman, Watson and Burke (1987).

This idea can be used both to observe and to share some literacy ideas with a beginning writer. Shared writing is a particularly useful way to observe the print knowledge of learners and can be introduced in many different situations to demonstrate aspects of written language to individual learners.

Resources needed Paper and pen or pencil

The experience You may wish to use this technique to evaluate a child's knowledge of written language, you might find the following approach helpful.

Invite the child to sit beside you and share your paper and pen. The basis of the activity is that you will provide a one-to-one demonstration of writing through your own model, with the child responding as he or she would in a spoken conversation. Explain that, instead of talking, today you are going to have a written conversation.

- First write, 'I'm ____' (your name), and as you write say what you are writing.
- Now invite the child to respond in writing and then read the response to you in turn. This will allow you to observe such features of the child's performance as:
  - knowledge of print directionality.
  - knowledge of print form of his or her own name, often the first thing learned. Does the child know the first letter, some letters, all letters?
  - ability to make use of grammatical structure provided, and read it ('I'm ____').
- Next write, 'I'm ____' (your age in numerals) and again read what you have written.
- Again invite the child to respond; this extends the above observations by providing some information about the child's knowledge of numerals.

This technique could be expanded very easily, if the child is able to cope with the above conversational gambits, to include questions such as 'Who is your best friend?' or 'What date is your birthday?'

- Now, for your turn, write 'I like to ____ (read, swim or other action)'.
- As the child responds, he or she will have the opportunity to try some more open-ended responses. You might also invite such a response by asking the question 'Why?'. If learners have difficulties in meeting your request, suggest they draw a picture of anything they are having trouble writing. This

Why is your cousin in hospital?

becks sha hs · got a

boto akal

How did she break her ankle?

she wo3 sat and

she tet is

Well, I hope she feels ~~feel~~ better

soon. I'ts been nice writing with you, Lizzie!

A conversation with Lizzie

technique encourages them to keep going, if some parts of the print task are beyond them.

This approach to sharing writing allows you to note:

- learners' willingness to take risks and try out new ideas, use of language, and spellings;
- their understanding of print directionality, concepts about words as indicated by their ability to separate words, and their knowledge of spelling;
- their pencil grip and letter formation.

An example of a written conversation is one with Lizzie who is an eight-year-old child who has recently begun to join in reading and writing experiences at school. Her responses during this written conversation demonstrate that she understands print directionality and has a knowledge of word concepts, and of print forms in general.

She demonstrates some beginning knowledge of spelling as she writes some letter sequences, and a willingness to take risks as she uses invented spelling. For example, she uses 'becks' to represent 'because' and 'akl' for 'ankle'. She shows an awareness of beginning and final sounds, demonstrating a very familiar spelling pattern used by many inexperienced writers, namely, she is much more aware of consonants than of vowels.

She uses conventional spelling when she has the teacher's model available. She gladly makes use of the teacher's closing remark, 'It's been nice writing with you.'

She makes appropriate responses to the language patterns used by her teacher.

CHAPTER 3

Helping inexperienced readers and writers

We have suggested that language is learned within the situations in which it is used, and that inexperienced and reluctant readers and writers must therefore be invited to engage in literacy in situations which are meaningful and relevant to them. As you demonstrate the spoken and written language appropriate to such situations and they are involved in using such language themselves, your students will learn about various aspects of language. They will also have an opportunity to think about the decisions that language users make as readers, writers, listeners and speakers.

A variety of situations are suggested for the opportunities they provide for children to visit and revisit literacy. These fall into three main categories:

1. Situations related to common social experiences so that learners will be encouraged to use literacy because they can see how literacy is useful to them as part of their daily lives. Importantly too, students have knowledge about such situations to support their efforts to read and write.
2. Situations which allow the sharing of stories and poems in ways which highlight the social aspects of reading. Such experiences allow learners to be involved in events and ideas which may be far removed from their daily lives and to enjoy what may be a whole new world.
3. Situations which emerge from across the curriculum and which involve the use of literacy as an integral part of the experiences available about the theme or topic.

Using experiences related to common social situations

Using environmental print

Fascinating accounts of young children exploring the written language that occurs in their world have been written by Baghban (1984), Bissex (1980) and Harste,

Woodward and Burke (1984). They provide very useful insights of ways in which children spontaneously link written language to the people and events in their lives.

Usually the first print symbols that children become aware of are letters in their own and their family members' names. As they explore the use of the print, they learn that written language is another way to 'say' things. The print found on road signs, packages and containers of all types, and so on, is directly related to the settings in which the print is found and is therefore highly predictable. Learners, if they are encouraged to do so and are not weighed down by a need to read and write conventionally, explore print occurring in various situations in their lives. They incorporate this way of representing their world just as they make use of colour, shape, movement, sound, and other features of their world.

The strategies used by young children provide us with a key to helping underachieving readers and writers become more aware of meaning–print relationships. We can help them to do so by encouraging them link to print what they know about the people and events happening in their daily lives. Reluctant readers and writers need encouragement to make these links, and we need to capitalize on every opportunity that arises in our daily classroom events to interest them in exploring written language. Some ways for encouraging learners to investigate print are outlined below.

Print on everyday packaging

You might wish to collect the labels from used food and other household packages and cans. Ask the learners in your class to bring along similar items from home. Magazines and newspapers are also useful resources for such print collections. Invite your students to sort these resources in various ways: things we like, things we keep in the bathroom and so on. Have them share their label collections with other children, discussing how they know the name of the object and sharing any clues they may have about the print. Some children will discuss where the package is kept or who uses the product. Others will refer to print such as letters or words they know, or even perhaps the unusual shape of the print. After this discussion, they might make individual books or charts about:

- their favourite foods.
- the things that are found in the laundry or kitchen.
- the things 'I like' or 'I need' or 'I want' (encourage them to incorporate these simple language structures into the book).

Alphabet frieze

Together with your students, you might prepare an alphabet frieze for a wall. This could incorporate product labels that begin with the different letters of the

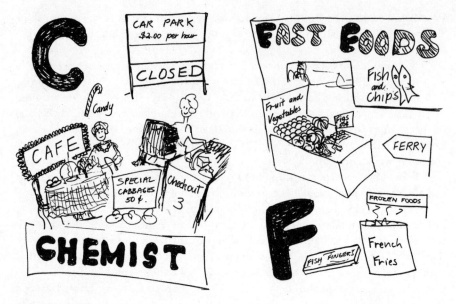

An alphabet frieze

alphabet. As the students add their labels to the frieze, discuss not only the different sound relationships that letters may have (e.g. *c*heese and *c*offee) but also the different visual appearance of the same letters (print) appearing on the different logos. They might enjoy inventing advertisements for their favourite products, and see how many words they can find to describe the item using words that begin with the same letter or rhyme. For example, 'Try tasty tangy twisters today.'

Have your students add their own names and those of their friends and other words they become interested in or need when writing, to the frieze. Older learners might add street names, TV characters' and pop-stars' names, and so on. Many poor readers and writers appear not to be interested in print relationships, and it is important to make their revisiting of print meaningful and purposeful. So have the students treat the frieze as a 'first dictionary' and use it as a resource when writing to the frieze.

Print we use for cooking

Recipes are a good example of the procedural texts we use every day to explain how to do things. They provide excellent reading experiences because they are so predictable since the text is about what is happening in the situation. Also the language structures used in recipes can be very simple and are similar to the language patterns we use every day: 'Do this', 'Get that'.

Invite your students to select a simple recipe for cooking and sharing. (Food such as hamburgers, pikelets, and tortillas are easy to prepare in a classroom, quick to cook, and can be made in an electric frying pan.) First, have the children decide what ingredients they will need and have them help you prepare a shopping list. The list should be recorded on a sheet of paper which is large enough for all to see what you are writing. Encourage them to look for the words they need in any resources in the classroom. This is also an opportunity to discuss the reasons why people write lists.

If possible, take the children with you on the shopping expedition. Have them identify items on the list and locate them in the shop. Encourage them to look for cues in the shop such as overhead signs and similar products which help them to locate the items. The children should be encouraged to use print information to confirm their guesses.

Have the recipe written out in advance on a large sheet of paper, leaving space beside each of the ingredients for the labels from appropriate packets and cartons to be added alongside. The instructions should be written in simple language such as that outlined below. Display your recipe prominently in the food-preparation area.

MEAT RISSOLES

You will need:

mince
salt
onion
1 egg
a little oil

1 knife
1 electric frying pan
1 spoon

1. Chop up the onion.
2. Mix the onion and mince, salt and eggs.
3. Heat up your pan.
4. Make the meat mixture into balls.
5. Fry gently until cooked.

It is helpful to have all the ingredients and utensils available on the table where everyone can see them. You might introduce the food preparation by discussing with the children what food might be made by using the ingredients and a frying pan. Then have them check with the title of the recipe to see who was correct. While many of them may not be able to read the words 'meat rissoles', they will be able to confirm whether their guesses are right using whatever print information they do know. You might also demonstrate to them some aspect of the relationship between sound and print symbol. 'Look – the word has an "r" at the beginning and an "s" in the middle. Listen – *risol*' (emphasizing these sounds in the word), and encourage the children to 'guess the word'.

The children can match the print on the labels of the ingredients with those on the recipe. Invite them to explain how they know the two words are the same although the print formats might be different. As you go on to each step in the recipe, first invite your students to predict what the next step might be, and then to confirm this by helping you read the recipe.

Sharing the food – writing invitations

You might wish to capitalize on the cooking lesson by allowing your students to invite a friend to join your class for lunch. Of course, such invitations would have to be written ones! Invite the students to suggest what information will be needed, and list this on the blackboard. They might say that their friends will need to know such information as:

- What is happening (lunch).
- Where (in my classroom).
- When (at 12.30 on Friday).
- Who is issuing the invitation.

After the children have thought through the function of the invitation, and you have demonstrated the written-language form, they can then decide how they will write their own invitations. Each child can prepare a written invitation for his or her friend. They have had the benefit of a demonstration of how to prepare an invitation and the situation itself provides the 'immersion' to help them be successful.

Print in our neighbourhood

You and your students might take a walk around the school grounds and in the immediate neighbourhood. All the children should have a pencil and paper to keep a record of any written language they see. A Polaroid camera (so teacher and children have an instant record to take back to the classroom) provides an invaluable resource of such experiences. Students might enjoy noting the different car makes, houses-for-sale signs, and other messages they spot. Before signs are recorded, have the students discuss with you or a friend what the print might say and how they know. 'It says "library". I know it is where all the books are kept. It starts with "l".' Encourage them to use their prior knowledge and to confirm with information from the print.

On your return to the classroom, have the students collaborate to recall the places you visited. As they do, you can demonstrate the written-language version of your excursion. Record this recount of their experience on a large sheet of paper placed where everyone can see what you are writing. Invite each child to provide an example of print collected and information about where it was found. For instance, the recount might read:

> On our walk Damien found a sign. It says 'Exit'. Then we saw the bakery. It had two signs saying 'Bakery' and 'Hot bread sold here'. We bought some. This is a label from a loaf of bread.

Such recounts are typical of the language which children use in their everyday ' lives as they tell about their past experiences. Of course, inexperienced literacy users will not necessarily be able to write such language conventionally from the start. However, they will benefit from the discussion and demonstrations of writing based on their personal experience. Of course, this will be just one of many experiences you can share with them, relating what they have been doing to the ways in which they can write about what has happened.

Linking talking and writing

Language experience approaches

Language-experience approaches to teaching reading and writing help to make written language very predictable. The written language transforms what learners know about and talk about into print. It is helpful to share reading and writing about situations occurring in the classroom when readers and writers are very inexperienced. The content of what is read and written will be known, and therefore predictable, to all the children.

Another strength of language experience is that we can capitalize on the language patterns of the children. Children typically use a limited range of grammatical structures (Hart and Walker 1977). This core of language patterns is used over and over again to provide the structure for communication in many different situations. These patterns are therefore predictable to inexperienced readers and writers because it is the core of spoken language.

A summary of some of the most common grammatical structures and the purposes for which they are used by speakers is set out in the table on page 20.

If you and the children are investigating rocks, or favourite stories, or ants, in your classroom, you can capitalize on these experiences to transform them from the spoken language you have used together in your discussion into written language. For example, after discussion about rocks you and the students might decide to record the experience in this way:

> I've got lots of rocks.
> I've got basalt and crystalline rocks.
> I found them on our walk.
> I like rock collecting.

Purpose for which the units are used	Focus on people	Focus on things
		That's [our dog]
Identification	I'm [Susan]	It's [Whiskers, a terrier]
Description	I'm [seven]	It's [brown]
Location	I'm [at home]	It's [in the garden]
Possession	I've got [freckles]	It's got [four legs]
Action	I'm [hopping]	It's [running]
State	I'm [happy]	It's [asleep]
Indicating	Look at [me]	Look at [it]
Likes	I like [my friend]	It likes [playing]
Needs	I need [a pencil]	It needs [water]
Wants	I want [my dinner]	It wants [some food]
Future intention	I'm going to [watch TV]	It's going to [for a walk]

(Items in square brackets are examples drawn from content. Hart and Walker 1984)

The content or field of the language is highly predictable to your students because it is part of their immediate experience. Alternatively, if the children are writing about their toys, the text might be:

> I've got lots of toys.
> I've got a bike and a chess game.
> I got them for my birthday.
> I like riding my bike and playing chess.

These grammatical structures can be introduced gradually, and should always be in an appropriate context. So they may use 'I like' to describe their feelings about swimming, TV and dogs. Similarly, 'I've got' might be used to discuss ownership of 'a TV' or 'a dog'. The language patterns remain constant, and only the content aspects are changed. The exploration of this language allows children to become familiar with the print forms of the language they speak every day. This provides them with access to a core of very useful written language.

Classroom experiences can be used as a basis for reading and writing based on this approach. You might, for example, grow plants, observe insects or go on an outing and then involve your students in writing about their experiences using this approach.

Growing plants   You might plant some mung beans, broad beans or other seeds that germinate and grow quickly. Such a situation provides opportunities for rosters for plant care. As you discuss with the children what needs to be done to look after the plants and record the growth and other observations, you can prepare a plant-care roster together. The roster will also provide a resource for children to refer to when writing about 'Our plant'.

	PLANT CARE ROSTER				
	Mon.	*Tues.*	*Wed.*	*Thurs.*	*Fri.*
Water the plants	Susan	Ian	Greg	Mike	Julie
Put them out in the sun		Maria			
Measure the plants			Tom	Anne	

For quick composition and immediate shared reading in your classroom you might wish to make grammatical-structure cards. These cards can be derived from those outlined on page 20, so the cards will consist of word clusters such as 'I'm', 'It's', 'I'm going to' and 'I've got'. With the children's help prepare content cards relating to the context about plants. You will need such content units as 'a plant', 'a root', 'some leaves', 'grow', 'water' and so on. These cards can then be used for quick composition, so that you and your students might use them to prepare a class report:

| I'm going to |——| grow |——| a plant |

| It's got |——| leaves |

As learners compose, they need to check each statement to make sure that it makes sense. However if someone attempts to combine the cards to read 'I'm a leaf', then the rest of the group should reject it. Similarly, if a child attempts to combine 'leaves grow it's got', then the discussion can be directed to whether 'we say things that way'. This strategy lesson introduces students to the need to attend to meaning and language based on an experience they know about and have discussed.

Of course, when your plants are ready, they will have to be eaten!

Linking language experience with informational books

One book which is a particularly useful extension is *Growing Radishes and Carrots* by Faye Bolton and Diane Snowball. This is a procedural text, somewhat like a recipe book, and it provides a series of directions on how to grow radishes, moving from 'Step 1: Dig the soil in the garden' to the final stage of pulling up the crop. The text then repeats the instructions for growing carrots, providing a further opportunity for readers who have difficulty with the first set of instructions, to cope the second time round.

You can plant some seeds in a container which is kept in a central place in your classroom where it is available for children to observe and record what happens. They might keep a simple diary together, with their own illustrations, to record the changes to the plants:

Week 1 The root began to grow.
Week 2 The root is longer.

The book, *Growing Radishes and Carrots*, has several interesting features, including a very simple table of contents and several diagrams. You would want to capitalize on these features, having learners reflect upon the ways in which such information helps them. The diagrams show the growth of the seeds and, if the experience is one which is happening in the classroom, the children can compare the diagram with the real-life event. Invite them to compare their own drawings with the one provided in the book, so they see how illustrations can help readers.

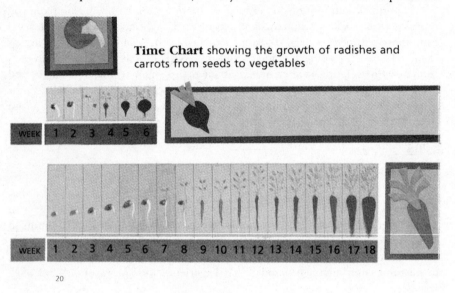

Time Chart showing the growth of radishes and carrots from seeds to vegetables

20

Growing radishes and carrots

With the children, construct a class time line of how long it took the class plants to grow, and compare this with the time charts in the book. Then with the children, develop a recount from their diaries which summarizes the experience. This is a good opportunity to talk about the connectives we use when writing to indicate the sequence of time over which events occurred.

RADISHES	CARROTS
In the first week the root began to grow.	*In the first week* the root did not grow.
By the second week the root was quite long.	*During the second week* we could see the tip of the root.
At the end of the sixth week the radishes were ready to eat.	The root continued to grow slowly *in the sixth week.*
	Finally, by week eighteen the carrots were ready to eat.

Most children should also be able to draw a number of conclusions by comparing the growth of the two types of plants. The text might be:

Radishes grow very quickly *compared with* carrots.
By the first week you can see the root of the radish, *but* the root of the carrot only appeared in the second week.
If you are hungry, it is *quicker* to grow radishes, *but* we like carrots *better*.

This text explores another way to organize information through language using comparison as a basis for organizing ideas in a factual text.

Exploring literature in the classroom

Reading stories to children and sharing literature with them are a most vital component in a programme designed to involve children in literacy. Through the process of sharing and the extended investigation of books they have an opportunity to enjoy stories and are invited to take part in the reading to the extent to which they are able. The process of sharing also provides teachers with an opportunity to demonstrate the strategies they use as readers when making decisions about what to read and how to read it. The procedure is explained in some detail below.

Predictable stories

In revisiting literature it is important to remember that all inexperienced readers need the support of highly *predictable* texts. These are predictable because of:

- recurrence of plot and characters.
- past experiences of the learners which have much in common with those in the text.
- repetitive language patterns.
- reinforcement of meaning and language through rhyme and rhythm.

There are many excellent books which have been specifically written for a younger audience. Books of this type are not so readily available for older children. However, it will be demonstrated that teachers can also invite older children to read such texts by suggesting that they approach these stories from perspectives appropriate to the children's own ages.

In exploring predictable books, there are three stages involved in sharing books:

- First of all, simply share the book with your class so that everyone can enjoy it.
- Next you will want to revisit the book so that your students can explore the special features of the text.

- Finally, you will want the children to use the text as a basis for further collaborative and personal responses.

Of course, not every book you share and enjoy together will be investigated in this depth. Some stories you will simply wish to read to the children for all to enjoy.

Sharing repetitive and cumulative plots

'I know an old lady', an old favourite, has a repetitive and cumulative plot and has been chosen to illustrate one way to share such stories. There is a big-book version of the story published by Ashton Scholastic which is a convenient way of sharing a book with a group of children. This story is one that is often popular with older inexperienced readers because of its humour, and they may even know it as a song. Because the language patterns are recurrent, the language becomes predictable, although it may be different from that used by the children everyday. Moreover rhyme and rhythm are strongly emphasized in the language. Therefore sharing it with inexperienced readers will offer excellent opportunities for them to become familiar with the patterns of plot, ideas, rhyme and rhythm used in written language. Soon they will be able to join in and read along.

Sharing the story   Show the book to the students and ask what they think the story might be about, given the information available from the title, the cover illustration and, of course, what they already know about stories in general, and this story in particular. A student might look at the cover illustration and predict that the story will be about an old lady who has trouble keeping flies out of her house. Others may read the title, using their print knowledge and the information available from the illustration. Encouraging students to predict in this way is very important, as you are demonstrating to them the process that readers naturally involve themselves in when they meet texts for the first time.

Invite your children to share what they know about the story and predict what they think might happen. You probably would not share the illustrations throughout the book before reading it, so you will keep the surprise twist of the story for the appropriate time.

As you share the story with the children, take care to highlight the dramatic content by using every available means of expression (inflection, volume, intonation, timing, and reference to illustrations), inviting them to enjoy the book with you. Encourage them to join in the reading and, should they not do so, you can issue invitations to them by, for example, pausing expectantly at appropriate points as the repetition reoccurs, such as: 'Perhaps ____?' or 'She swallowed the spider to ____.'

Revisiting the story   After the shared reading, use the illustrations as a source of reference, as the children decide why the incidents happened in the order they did. This should lead to a discussion of the ways in which the various animals are related. The dog is swallowed after the cat; ask the children why this might have happened. Again, why did the cat swallow the bird?

You might also discuss the differences between what happened in the story and what the children predicted might happen before you shared the book.

Now reread the book. This time indicate the words in the text which you are reading with a sweep of your hand or a ruler to demonstrate to the children print concepts such as top to bottom, left-to-right progression, left page before right, and that print is a major source of attention.

Children can also be encouraged to make use of any relevant sound-symbol knowledge to confirm information in the illustrations and from the rhyme and rhythm patterns. Some of the children may predict, if you pause after you have read, 'Who swallowed a cat, Fancy ____', that the next word is 'that'.

As you reread the story, you might also pause at appropriate points to make comments such as: 'The old lady's problem is really getting serious now, isn't it? She's swallowed a spider, a bird, a cat and a dog to try to solve it, but things just seem to be getting worse! I wonder what else she might do?'

As you share your strategies as a reader in this way, you are demonstrating the kind of thinking that readers use while reading. You are demonstrating how you relate information from the text to what you know about stories. Sharing a text with your children will also provide you with an excellent opportunity to discuss with them unusual language patterns which may be found in books but which are not common in everyday language, e.g. 'How absurd to swallow a bird.' These demonstrations are important in helping children to learn what readers do, as many of them may be unaware of information in print.

Personal responses: for younger learners   Ask the children to select one of the episodes that happened in the story and illustrate by drawing or painting their favourite. Where one child might choose to make a drawing of the old lady swallowing a dog, another might illustrate her as she swallows a spider. Have them order their pictures into a sequence and explain why they have selected the sequence they did. Their story might have a different order from that in the original story, and you might together write a class story about the new version.

> I know an old lady
> Who swallowed the dog.
> She swallowed the dog,
> To catch the cow.
> She was hungry.

You can also use the opportunity to share your writing strategies with the children. For instance, you might read what you have written aloud, and then decide to change a word because another one would be better. Explain to the children the reasons for your change. You might also involve them in helping with some print decisions that arise during the writing, such as the initial letter of a word or whether you should use a capital or a lower-case letter.

Personal responses: for older learners   To ensure that older learners will be willing to remain engaged in the exploration of the book, it is important to establish the fact that this book is read and enjoyed by people of all ages. Open the discussion by inviting the children to look for the name of the author. Ask them whether, in their opinion, the author would be more likely to be an adult or a child. They will almost certainly agree that the author would have been an adult who is writing for children. As you share the story with your students, have them decide why younger children would find the story humorous.

After you have shared the story together, you might involve the children in shared writing with a view to writing a new version for younger children. You might prepare a 'skeleton text' of the repetitive language patterns on large sheets of white paper:

> *I know an Old _____.*
>
> I know an old _____,
> Who swallowed a _____,
> But I don't know why
> _____ swallowed the _____,
> Perhaps _____ die.
>
> I know an old _____,
> Who swallowed a _____,
>
> _____
>
> _____.
>
> _____ swallowed the _____
> To catch the _____,
> But I don't know why
> _____ swallowed the _____,
> Perhaps _____ die.

Now demonstrate for the children the various strategies you would use in filling in the skeleton. You might, for example, brainstorm aloud ideas for different story characters and settings. List these ideas on the blackboard:

CHARACTER	SETTING	ANIMALS
fisherman	the sea	shrimp crab fish octopus shark whale

Now have the children help you identify some other sets:

CHARACTER	SETTING	ANIMALS
hunter	jungle	worm frog snake
		monkey tiger elephant
witch	dungeon	bug lizard bat rat hound
		dragon

This allows you to discuss an important aspect of cohesion in text, i.e., if the story is to 'hang together', then the words that you include will be related.

Next, you need to explain how you will have to order the animals so that each will be small enough to be devoured by the next. You might go on by thinking aloud through your choices in this way:

> Let's see... I know an old witch... *Yes!* I like that. A witch would probably live in a cave or a dungeon, wouldn't she?... Now let's see, what could we make an old witch swallow?... a dragon would be an excellent big creature for her... what would be some other nasties? Rats, bugs, lizards, *bats*... ah yes! Something bigger... hounds, cats...

Now you are ready to begin writing:

> I know an old witch
> Who swallowed a bug,
> But I don't know why
> She swallowed the bug.
> Perhaps she'll die.

You might also demonstrate ways of identifying rhymes, so that you are highlighting aspects of sound-symbol relationships, i.e., sometimes rhyming words look alike and at times they do not:

bat	cat	why	fly
mat	that	die	sigh

These listings can be kept and added to as other examples arise.

Then you might demonstrate how you use this information:

> Let's see now, I need two more lines, and this [indicating the highlighted blank] must rhyme with this word, 'bat'. How'll I do that? I know... I'll write down all of the words I know that *do* rhyme with 'bat'...
>
> Now, the lines that we write *must* make sense as well as rhyme with 'bat'...
>
> We could say 'Imagine that, she swallowed a bat', but I don't want to do that because that was in the original story... what about... Crunch, munch, *splat!* She swallowed a bat... *yes!* I like that.

Now the children will be ready to write their own or a group version of the fate of some other character. If you have a brainstorming session first, and as you record their ideas, you can demonstrate and discuss spelling. Encourage the students to use invented spelling, which is the use of any pattern which will allow them to identify the word later, so that they keep their ideas flowing while they continue writing. You can discuss such spellings with the children when they have finished their draft.

Stories based on familiar ideas

There is a good range of books which are predictable because they are based on cyclical events. Days of the week and the seasons of the year, number patterns and colours have all been used to provide a pattern which is predictable for learners once they have recognized what the pattern is that the author is using.

Sharing the story   Younger children who need a special invitation to become involved in books usually enjoy Eric Carle's *The Very Hungry Caterpillar*. They will need you to share several pages of the book with them in the same way that has been suggested above in the sharing of 'I know an old lady'. But then many of them will be able to join in as they recognize the pattern, 'On Monday he ate...', and will 'read', i.e., make reasonable use of the illustrations to help them take care of the rest of the caterpillar's menu. You will probably be the major reader of the conclusion, until the children have shared the book several times.

Older reluctant readers can become engaged if they are encouraged to consider the possibilities for writing spoofs in the ways discussed above in 'I know an old lady'.

Revisiting the story   It might be useful to use a coloured highlighter to emphasize the words that represent the changing words that appear in the repetitive parts of this story. As the children move more independently to 'read' the text, using mainly the illustrations, you and they might discuss how a reader knows the word is 'strawberry', for example, and not 'plum', using the clues that are available both in the illustration and the print.

Have the children brainstorm other objects the caterpillar might eat, and list these on the board, discussing some aspects of spelling strategies that writers use as you do so. For example, the children might suggest:

leaves
lettuce
tomatoes
potatoes

(The last two words might be discussed – look at the pattern '-toes' at the end, or the way both of the first words begin with 'le-' and yet they do not sound the same.)

Invite the children to change the objects the caterpillar ate by drawing pictures of the objects and appropriate word cards which can be attached to the book using blu-tack. They and their friends can share their new story.

The children might enjoy writing and illustrating their own books about the things that were eaten. The possibilities of 'The very hungry goat' or 'The very hungry whale' might, for example, be explored.

Variations can also be introduced such as 'On the first day', 'At one o'clock', 'In January'...

For older children   Older reluctant writers might be interested in writing a story for younger children.

> On Monday Caspar the friendly ghost
> flew through the wall
> but he couldn't find his shadow.
>
> On Tuesday Caspar the friendly ghost
> flew over the roof
> but he couldn't...

The students can illustrate the new version with appropriate cut-outs, using the split-page format used in the original story.

Repetitive language patterns

There are a number of other stories which allow opportunities for children to explore other language patterns. One very well-known story, for example, is Eric Carle's *The Mixed-up Chameleon*. It is one older children will enjoy with its delightful drawings and humorous story line.

Sharing the story   You might wish to begin by discussing what a chameleon is. You might also talk about camouflage and other animals that protect themselves the way the chameleon does.

As you share the story with your children, they will become attuned to the patterns of language – 'If I could be like a...'. As they recognize the repetitive patterns of language used by the chameleon, together with the prompts provided by the pictures, they will be able to join you in the reading. As you turn the pages, invite the children to identify the animal and predict what each might want to do – 'a giraffe, it's got a long neck – the chameleon will want to reach up very high' – then together you can read the author's version.

Invite the children to guess what the chameleon will look like by the end of the book before sharing the ending.

Revisiting the story   Reread the story with the children, asking them to suggest other things that might happen if the chameleon's wishes were to come true. For example,

> If I could be like the elephant, then I could drink without bending my head.
>
> If I could be like the elephant, then I could swing my trunk.

These extra ideas could be written on cards, and with blu-tack, added to the appropriate pages.

Inviting a personal response   Children might write their own personal wish books. 'If I could be like... [an acrobat, an astronaut], then I would be...', based on the language patterns of the story.

You might wish to use these ideas with other stories which have a similar pattern.

Linking personal experiences with story plots

It is important that children are provided with opportunities to link their personal experiences with the episodes that take place in stories. Stories such as Pat Hutchins's *Rosie's Walk*, which is based upon Rosie's journey, are excellent resources to introduce such links to excursions you take with the children. Such an excursion could be a treasure trip around the school, a bus trip to local or neighbouring places of interest, and so on.

Planning an excursion

Before setting out on the excursion, have the children think about the reasons for the outing. Children's purposes must be related to the situation so, if the excursion is a treasure hunt, the purpose may be to find Easter eggs. Then you can assist them to design a means of recording their experiences.

Very young children might simply carry paper and pencil to draw pictures of the number of eggs they find, and where they find them. Later they can use this information to help them recount the events of their Easter-egg hunt. You can support this recount by first writing a class account of the excursion:

> Mrs Jones's class went on an egg hunt
> around the library
> past the swings
> through the adventure playground...

Then you might discuss other places where the children found eggs, and list these:

> classroom
> tennis court
> office

as a resource for children to consult as they extend their written recounts of the egg hunt. The children can also draw a map of the school grounds showing where the eggs were found.

Older children might like to draw up a check list of all the places they intend to search, and to record their successes or failures with ticks, numerals or even a bar graph.

Linking classroom experience with the story

The account of *Rosie's Walk* can be linked with the class egg hunt as both involve an account of what happened during an excursion.

Sharing the book   *Rosie's Walk* by Pat Hutchins provides a resource for many useful learning experiences, as it is a simple story about a not terribly intelligent hen's journey around the farmyard. Rosie is totally oblivious of events happening around her, and in particular of the fox lurking in the background. One of the most interesting features of the book is the way the author has chosen to use the illustrations to 'tell the story', while the written language provides only a prosaic account of where Rosie went.

First of all, share the illustrations with the children and discuss what can be seen in each. Invite the children to predict what might happen to Rosie and the fox.

As you read the book to the children invite them to join in and suggest what place they think Rosie will visit next; for example, after you have read the first few pages, they might be able to guess that Rosie walked 'across the hay' or 'around the windmill'.

When the story reading is complete, discuss how the fox is foiled in each episode. You might also discuss whether the children would have preferred to have the story of the fox and Rosie told by the author, rather than through the illustrations.

Revisiting the story   Give the children the book and a large sheet of paper, and have them sketch where they think the places are located that Rosie passed by during her walk. As they revisit the story, they may find they will need to alter some of their map, particularly if they do not allow for the fact that Rosie starts and finishes at the chicken coop. When their map is complete, they can use paint and collage to complete the illustration of the places Rosie visited. Ice-lolly sticks can be used for the fence, wisps of grass for the haystack, and so on.

Then the children can reread the book and decide where to put in trackmarks of Rosie's journey. They can also draw or trace around pictures of Rosie and the fox to create puppets for story retelling.

After the children have shared the story telling and are familiar with the episodes, you might revisit the story again. Pause at relevant points and write labels on each location card. Have the children place these on the appropriate spots on their map. Involve the children in discussion as to how they can recognize the words on the cards, using initial or final letters to help them. You might also discuss irregularities such as those involved in 'chicken coop'.

The children can then write an account of Rosie's adventures, telling what is revealed in the illustrations rather than in the text. For example:

> Rosie walked over the haycock.
> Then the fox jumped on to the haycock
> and grabbed Rosie, but he
> fell into the haycock. CRASH!

The children could then share their new version of the story.

Rosie What for a wock arend the gard she wock ofa The rack and he fox pest on the rack and ot het in the hos bi the fack Rosie wrod of a the haestac The fox pent in the haestac Rosie

A child's response to Rosie's Walk

Linking Rosie's Walk *to the egg hunt* If we return to the children's accounts of the egg hunt, they might enjoy adding a character who accompanied them on their egg hunt in the same way as the fox joined Rosie. They could return to their sketch of the egg-hunt journey, recalling where they went from their written recounts. Each location can be on a separate page. Then they can decide who might have pursued them – perhaps a fox or a giant, or any other character they choose. They might then extend their original account in writing too:

> Mrs Jones's class went on an egg hunt
> around the library.
> The giant crept along behind them.
>
> When the children went past the swings
> the giant hid behind the tree...

Moving on   The children might also write about other adventures of Rosie the hen, or of other characters such as Mollie the mouse or William the worm. In this way the children will have the chance to try out the knowledge they have gained through their previous experiences to write their new version.

To prepare the children to create their own texts, you could explore the hunter–prey concept which underlies the story of Rosie and the fox. The children can relate this to other animals or perhaps to cartoons they may have seen. Invite the children to identify other animal hunters and prey. This information can be recorded under headings as a data bank to provide a resource for the children's future writing:

Hunter	Prey	Location
cat	mouse	house, barn
lion	zebra	Africa
wolf	sheep	field
bird	worm	grass
Tom	Jerry	house

Before the children begin their writing, you might write a class story together. Have them decide upon a hunter and prey, and then sketch a scene. If you decide to use the cat–mouse combination, you might model a kitchen, with a stove, a refrigerator, table, chairs, sink, cupboard, kettle. The children will help you.

Then you could 'think aloud' as you decide details such as choosing the mouse's name, perhaps enhancing this by using alliteration.

> Let's see... Freddie the mouse? Heather the mouse? No. I think I like Molly the mouse! It sounds better, doesn't it, because *M*olly and *M*ouse start with the same sound and the same letter.

The children might help you decide how a mouse would move by running, scampering or creeping. Then you might invite them to help you to decide whether the mouse would creep over the chair or around the cupboard. When you have all determined which route your mouse is going to take, the children can then think about ways that the mouse might escape each time the cat attempts to pounce. The model will help them with these decisions.

As each episode is composed, you can write the text on a large sheet of white paper. When you have finished, have the children help you reread it and decide upon any changes that should be made to the language (editing), and the spelling and punctuation (proofreading). This provides a useful demonstration of the writing process.

Now the children can create their own versions. The less confident ones may wish to refer back to the list of hunters and their prey they prepared previously. Invite them to choose characters and a setting to write about. Each of them can model their own pair of characters and props from plasticine, or sketch a setting for their story. The stories, when complete, can be published and illustrated, and shared with other children.

Further extensions   To extend the plot of the journey, some children might enjoy reading the predictable old favourite 'In a dark dark wood' (one version is retold by June Melser and Joy Cowley), and then perhaps write an alternative version. The predictability of this story rests on the relationships existing in a situation. In this instance there is the wood–path–house–stair and so on. You might invite the children to develop a similar pattern of places:

> school
> path
> classroom
> corner
> cupboard
> ____

and invite them to think of some unusual twist that they might write around the setting. They might suggest having a story character appear or yet another ghost! The choice is theirs, and the simple repetitive language can be altered to suit the new story.

Another story which has a similar story structure is *Mr Smudge's Thirsty Day* by Jonathon Gunson. Similarly, stories like *The Big Toe* by Joy Cowley which tells of the search by something looking for its big toe, and *Dan, the Flying Man*, also by Joy Cowley, provide opportunities for children to read more or less independently, supported by their experiences with similar stories.

An excellent book with a similar theme to that existing in *Rosie's Walk* (fox hunting hen) is *Hattie and the Fox* by Mem Fox. This story also has a very predictable cumulative structure. If you read the first three pages with them, the children will be able to help you 'read' the rest, with perhaps an occasional invitation to look at the illustrations to confirm what other part of the fox can be seen. This book also lends itself to choral reading, with different members of the class taking responsibility for each animal.

Another book you might wish to read to your students is *Fox Eyes*, a story written by Margaret Wise Brown and beautifully illustrated by Garth Williams. But, where the fox in *Rosie's Walk* is present only in the pictures, in this story the journey of the fox and the reactions of the other animals are documented through the language as well as the illustrations. The children might enjoy comparing the different ways in which the authors and illustrators of the two books have told their stories. They might also like to compare the characters of the foxes and the havoc caused by them in the two stories.

And doubtless you have a variety of favourite books of this type that you share with the children to create links between their own experiences and those of story characters.

Linking personal experience with the language of stories

It is important that inexperienced literacy learners see how their own experiences can be recaptured in the language other authors use in writing stories. Their writing about growing plants (see pages 21–3) might, for example, be extended into a 'Great big enormous turnip' story. Share a version of this traditional story with the children. One version which involves nursery-rhyme characters is *The Great Big Enormous Watermelon* by Brenda Parkes and Judith Smith.

Then have a number of sheets of white paper ready and, with the help of the children, prepare a version of this story based upon the class plant.

> Once upon a time we planted a seed.
> Every day we watered it.
> Julie watered the plant.
> Luigi watered the plant.
>
> Each day our plant grew and grew and grew.
> One day, it grew *so big*,
> it was ready to eat...

Encourage the children to make use of the repetition of language and print. The children might use coloured pens in their writing to emphasize the repetitions in the language; for example, have the children write the refrain 'watered the plant' in green, and the repetition of the word 'grew' in yet another colour. Print-format features such as size, shape, and colour, can be used to highlight the intonation patterns used by people when telling stories. For instance, people will emphasize the '*so big*' as they read, and the children can indicate this by the size and shape of the print they use as they write.

You might prepare cardboard covers for the book. When the story is complete, have the children decide upon an appropriate title and how they will illustrate the cover. They should also add their names as authors. When the story is illustrated, it can be added to the class library and also borrowed by children to take home and share with their families.

Another experience   Wordless books such as Tomie de Paola's book *Pancakes for Breakfast* can provide another opportunity to link classroom events with stories. This book has no print except for the pancake recipe and the occasional sign.

You might introduce Tomie de Paola's book by first making pancakes using the recipe included in the book. If the directions are written up on a large chart and displayed on the wall near the cooking area, then your students will be able to 'read and make'. You might wish to follow the procedures discussed earlier in this chapter (pages 16–18).

Afterwards, share the wonderful illustrations in de Paola's book with the children and invite them to tell the story. Have the children suggest names for the characters and talk about ways in which they might describe them. They might call the lady 'the little old woman' or 'Mrs Giovanni' and so on. How would they describe her – 'jolly', 'plump' – and her clothes? Discuss each of the illustrations in turn, inviting the children to suggest how they would write the story.

Record the storytelling. Use a separate sheet to correspond with each page in the book so that the children can match their story with the pictures. If you have two copies of the book and are willing to separate the pages, you have the basis for a wonderful wall story. The illustrations can be hung up around the room with the matching texts below:

> One winter, early in the morning, the sun rose above the hill near a little house. It was very cold. It had snowed all night.
>   Slowly Mrs Giovanni opened one eye, and then the other. Her dog Bittzer lay on the floor, and her fat cat woke up.

The children will then have an interesting story that they have written to share with visitors to the room and you might invite the children to relate the stories that can be told about other wordless books.

Linking conversation with the language of books

Much of our everyday language is conversational – people talking to one another and asking questions. There are a number of excellent books which pick up this pattern of language and provide resources which are very useful for inexperienced readers.

Sharing

One such question and answer book provides an introduction to legends and myths. *Where does the sun go at night?* by Mirra Ginsburg speculates on the fate of the sun each night, with each response followed by a further question. We find out, for example, that the sun goes to his grandma's house, but the question 'Where does he sleep?' immediately follows. This book, or one similar to it, provides learners with an opportunity to visit written language which uses the same form as much of their own spoken language.

As you read the questions, the children in your class could be encouraged to predict possible answers, for example, where does the sun sleep at night – in the clouds, in the sky, or in a bed? Involve the children in following up their predictions by reading to confirm – 'in his grandma's bed'. Most would be able to read 'in his... bed'. But some may not be able to read 'grandma' and you can decide together whether this matters. As the children read on, they will find it does, because the word occurs again immediately. So then children will have to follow through by looking at the pictures and looking for any clues in the print. This, of course, provides an important strategy lesson about the need to make use of all the information possible during reading.

Revisiting and personal responses

After one or two readings you and the children might decide to innovate on the text, and create a legend of your own. Ask the children to suggest ideas for other innovations, for instance 'Where do birds go in winter?' or 'Where do whales go all year round?'

List the children's suggestions about the selected theme.

Where do birds go in winter?

---

warm places
live in trees

This will form the basis for an expanded version to be written by individual children or groups of children:

Where do birds go in winter?

Where do birds go in winter? They fly to warmer places.
Where do they live? In their mother's trees near the sea.
Who is their mother? The sun and the rain.

The finished book or books could be edited and illustrated. The preparation of the final copy could provide an opportunity to discuss punctuation, such as the role of question marks. Have the author or authors read their questions and have other children respond. Then the children can decide upon the necessary punctuation.

Encouraging students to become more independent

You may wish to extend this question and answer genre by exploring other similar books. One factual book which makes use of the same format of question and answer is *Where Does the Butterfly Go when It Rains?* by May Garelick. The author's use of rhyme and rhythm is helpful too in making readers aware of these features of language. The delicate, somewhat muted, illustrations also provide a wealth of information to support a reader in search of meaning.

You might first share the title and cover illustration with your students. It might also be useful to select one or two of the rhymes from this book and discuss cloze responses for them before sharing the book so that they will be confident to use rhyme and rhythm clues when they join in the reading. For example, have the children decide what the missing words might be in the following rhymes:

> A rabbit can dash whoosh
> – into a ____
>
> I would know what to do
> in the rain, wouldn't ____

When you read the book, pause when rhymes occur in the text and invite the children to predict from such aspects of language.

Where pages end with a question, invite your class to speculate on possible responses. Then compare the writer's answer with what the children have thought might happen, without holding up the reading to a point where the storyline gets lost.

When you have read through the book, you and the children might again explore the illustrations and see how these hold the answers to many of the questions.

Invite the children to write their own accounts about what people and animals do on rainy days. Some children will probably want to pose their own questions such as 'Where do rainbows end?' or 'Why do frogs croak?'

You might begin with the children brainstorming ideas on the subject:

> *On rainy days*
>
> people run
> people shiver
> birds are silent
> But ducks are happy.

Strongly patterned books like these do provide reluctant writers with excellent models to try out their ideas. Of course, most important of all is an audience of readers who respond enthusiastically to what the children have written.

Question and answer books of facts   It can be difficult to find simply written reference books that can be used by reluctant older readers. One solution is, of course, to develop gradually a class library of books written by your own students.

You might start out by offering two books of this type to the students to read independently. The first of these is *Tails* by Marcia Vaughan. This is a book of questions, and highly predictable because of the illustrations which also provide the answers. For example, there is a picture of a pig's tail, with the question 'Whose tail is curly?' Students might enjoy creating similar books on other topics – faces, rocks, bikes, or any topic that is of interest to them. Illustrations could include the opportunity to use collage techniques.

Another book, *Breathing* by Honey Andersen, poses a series of questions, 'Do _____ breathe through noses and mouths?', with the next page providing the response 'No! _____ breathe through their _____.' The text is cumulative in so far as the question is framed from the previous response, therefore helping the reader to predict. It also provides excellent opportunities for discussion about the repetition of print. Again, your students might enjoy creating books of this type.

Exploring literacy throughout the curriculum

The opportunities for students to learn literacy and about literacy are ongoing throughout the school day. Good readers and writers are encouraged to use their literacy knowledge to learn. Unfortunately the less able students often have fewer opportunities to read and write about the areas of the curriculum because of the lack of suitable resources and their unwillingness to 'have a go'.

Incorporating science into the literacy programme

Reports are a helpful type of text through which to introduce the less able students to the writing of factual information. Reports usually consist of a general statement about the field (i.e. the topic) which is then followed by a series of supporting statements. The language is therefore usually a monologue, and written in present continuous tense:

> Trees are very large plants. Some lose their leaves each year. Others keep their leaves. They are called evergreens.

A number of report-type books, suitable for inexperienced readers, have been published recently. These can be used to introduce readers to reports as well as providing excellent resources for incorporating reading and writing into the curriculum. Examples of some of the titles are:

Trucks by John and Yvonne Pollock
Animal Mothers and Babies by Judith Smith and Brenda Parkes
Chickens by Diane Snowball

A unit on the life-cycle

Sharing   To provide experience with observing a life-cycle you may have the children observe how tadpoles turn into frogs or how silkworms hatch. Such experiences provide children with the necessary knowledge and involve them in writing and reading for reasons which are relevant to them. It is also much easier to create relevant purposes for reading and writing which will invite reluctant learners to participate if these are related to the situation that is going on in your classroom.

An excellent resource to share with the children is *Tadpole Diary* by David Drew. This book is in a diary form. There is also a section containing information about caring for tadpoles. The contents page and index are also very useful resources for introducing children to the help these book-format features can provide. The tables and illustrations also provide useful models of these book features.

You might first involve your students in observing and recording the changes at each stage. The text might be something along these lines:

Week 1:   We found frogs' eggs in the creek. We put seven frogs' eggs in a jar of water.
Week 2:   Three eggs hatched. The tadpoles began to swim.
Week 3:   All the eggs have hatched. The tadpoles are getting bigger.

Involve the children in sketching the changes in the animals, and in estimating the changes in size. These records could be added to the report.

Then each week you might compare your class observations with what is recorded in the book – the big-book version of *Tadpole Diary* would be most useful here. The children might like to incorporate the labelling used in the book into their own observations and compare their specimens with the photographs and illustrations in the book.

Use the contents page to invite the children to find the information about tadpoles and frogs, and see whether they would wish to add further information to the class report. Again, when your frogs have hatched, compare the life-cycle of your tadpoles and frogs with the diagram and information contained in the book. The children should also use the contents page to locate the information about caring for tadpoles.

If the children raise questions that they cannot answer, invite them to use the index to find the answers to their questions.

When the class tadpoles have hatched, you might involve the children in writing a report based on their observations and reading as on the facing page.

Other resources   You might wish to introduce the other books in the same series as

---

FROGS AND TADPOLES

The frog lays eggs in a pond.
The eggs float on the water.
The eggs hatch out and they are tadpoles.

The tadpole grows for several days...

Tadpole Diary (*The Life of the Butterfly*, *Caterpillar Diary*, and *Animal Clues*) as these fit into the experiences you are sharing with the children in your class. They will provide the children with further experiences of simple factual writing and of the non-print features that frequently accompany such texts, such as diagrams, line drawings and so on.

Animal Mothers and Babies (Smith and Parkes 1984) is another simple report which discusses four different animals: the cat, the hen, the kangaroo, and the turtle. The information about each animal is the same:

• description
• feeding and care
• protection

except for the turtle, which the text explains is different.

You might begin by discussing with the children what they know about cats. You might list on the board some of the words that the children use, as the opportunity also provides the chance to talk about the spelling decisions at the same time.

CATS AND KITTENS

Description	*Feeding and care*	*Protection*
furry	milk	growls
soft	meat	spits

Share the first pages with the children. Then discuss the information in the illustrations which accompany the text about the hen and chickens. Invite your students to try to read the next four pages independently, reminding them that the information will probably be about description, feeding and care, and protection, since this is what the illustrations reflect.

A word riddle   You might prepare a cloze-type task for the next four pages of the book *Animal Mothers and Babies*, covering several of the words with small slips of card attached with blu-tack. You might, for instance, cover the word 'hungry' and invite the children to predict what the word is, treating the task as a guessing

The mother cat looks after her kittens.
She licks them when they are dirty.
She plays with them too.

Animal mothers and babies (a)

But when the baby turtles hatch
they are all alone.
Their mother has gone.

Animal mothers and babies (b)

game or riddle. They will have clues from the words 'feeds', 'drinks' and 'milk' which are all part of the chain of information relating to food needs. When the children uncover the word, they can confirm or disconfirm their guess using graphophonic clues. If the children have predicted other words such as 'thirsty' or 'tired', invite them to explain why they predicted these words. Do not dismiss their answers as wrong, but use the opportunity to compare the different answers – and you may be surprised at the very good reasons children will give for their choices.

Another cloze deletion might be of pronouns such as 'it' – 'the mother kangaroo looks after her joey. She plays with _____ too.' Here children may suggest 'the joey', 'it' or indeed something else. Again the discussion is as important as the confirmation of the response, and the children will have been invited to reflect on the use of personal pronouns which are important resources of reference in text.

Comparisons The information about the turtle in the book *Animal Mothers and Babies* presents a contrasting picture as the baby turtle has to care and fend for itself in comparison with the other animals described previously. This is highlighted by a print-format feature in the book involving the use of bold print. You might read the first page with the children and discuss the print type and reasons why it might have been chosen to highlight the comparison. Encourage the children to explain how this warns readers that something is going to be different.

After you have shared the book, the children might describe other animals and their needs for care and protection, and create data banks dealing with this information.

	Description	Care	Protection
Frogs	slippery green long legs	feed themselves	look after themselves

Children will probably enjoy writing and illustrating their own animal mothers and babies books. The data banks will help them organize their ideas and also be a reference for their print decisions as writers.

Incorporating social occasions into the literacy programme

Social occasions in the classroom can provide excellent opportunities for children to explore a variety of functions for the use of written language, and the related ways in which language is used in each of such texts.

A celebration

Children and parents enjoy joining in celebrating special occasions such as class days or days which are special in other cultures. One such celebration is the Chinese New Year.

Children need to talk a lot about the New Year experiences they have enjoyed, and then to discuss the special customs of the Chinese at the New Year. They can make New Year greeting cards, and they might ask some friends to join them for a meal for the occasion, requiring the preparation of invitations.

Have the children choose from a selection of greeting cards to decide how they would design their own cards. Of course, this involves considerable reading and discussion. The card collection can be available as a resource for the children as they make their own cards.

The children can prepare invitations for their friends. They will probably need help in thinking through the information that needs to be included, such as:

- Who is being invited.
- Who is doing the inviting.
- When and where the occasion is to be held.
- The nature of the occasion.

The children can also make paper lanterns for decorations. Write out directions for making the lanterns and make a lantern as a model. If the directions are simple and include some illustrations, and the children have a lantern as a model, they are able to make their own lanterns fairly independently of you.

MAKING PAPER LANTERNS

1 sheet of paper
Scissors
Staples

1. Cut a strip of the paper about 3cms wide.
2. Fold the rest of your paper in half.
3. Cut nicks in the paper along the crease.
4. Now open out the paper.
5. Staple the edges of the paper together.
6. Staple on the strip of paper to the top as a handle.

The children can help you decide upon a menu and help prepare the food for the party. Afterwards, the children can write out the recipes to share with their families and friends, involving them in further experiences with procedural language.

Exploring language through literacy

Poetry has a great deal to offer language learners of all ages. Very young children learn about the rhymes, rhythms and the structures of story language from nursery rhymes and other simple, repetitive verses. Older children need to be encouraged to enjoy the sounds, sights and meanings that poetry evokes. Poetry writing offers unique opportunities to make underconfident readers and writers more aware of the sounds of language.

Nursery rhymes and younger children

When beginning primary school, some children come to school displaying language delays. Whatever the cause of such delays, we must provide opportunities for such children by revisiting the natural kinds of parent–child experiences which ensure language growth for most children. Parents and young children share nursery rhymes in a warm, intimate setting. The parent usually enhances the language situation by making effective use of voice intonation and volume, timing and tapping that highlight rhyme and rhythm and reflect the way in which the writer develops the story line in many nursery rhymes. Teachers should also provide these experiences.

So invite your children into an area of your classroom where you and they can share some of the closeness and comfort that exist in family reading situations. Large cushions for the children and a low chair for you help to set the scene. Have your nursery rhyme available in big-print format so that all the children can see it from where they are sitting. Some publishers have printed poems in big-book formats (such as *Gobble Gobble Glup Glup* and the *Beginnings Poster Book*, with poems and nursery rhymes selected by Brenda Parkes and Judith Smith). These big books make the process of sharing much more feasible. Small-book collections such as Nicola Bayley's *Book of Nursery Rhymes* are ideal for sharing with one or two children.

You might share a rhyme such as 'This little pig' using a poster format. Highlight recurring elements in the language by writing the repetitive parts in a way that emphasizes the repetitions, e.g. through use of colour or print-format features:

> *This little pig* went to market,
> *This little pig* stayed at home,
> *This little pig* had roast beef,
> and *this little pig* had none,
> and *this little pig* went *wee-wee-wee* all the way home.

First, you might invite the children to suggest who or what this nursery rhyme is going to be about. You could ask the children where the little pig might go. If the little pig stayed at home, what would he do? This sharing of information helps to provide them with ideas about what might be in the rhyme.

Then read the text with appropriate drama, intonation and rhythm. Discuss what happened to the pigs.

Reread the poem several times, using a pointer to show the print-directionality features. Talk about which way we read print, and emphasize the break at the end of each line as you drop down to the next. Then, if you think the children would enjoy this, invite different children to show the others where to read. The child-as-teacher can use the pointer to show the others where to read.

The children can also dramatize the story while someone else acts as narrator.

You might also share the print features, referring to the words such as 'this little pig' which occur again and again. The children might enjoy suggesting who else could be in the nursery rhyme. They could replace, for example, 'this little pig' with their own names – you can use small cards with their names and blu-tack to attach the cards to the appropriate places. As each child is given or writes personal name cards, talk to them about some feature of the print in their names, 'Look, Sharon, your name starts with an "S".' Children can take turns to put their name cards on as the others read the poem.

After a number of sharings the children might enjoy changing 'this little pig' to 'this little duck' or 'this little frog' and so on, and end up with a new nursery rhyme. The use of the phrase cards as suggested above is a quick way for them to do so. Of course, you might model the print for the first card and invite them to write the other cards they will need for their turn.

To emphasize rhythm you can also use music for those nursery rhymes that can be sung. March with them as you sing 'The grand old Duke of York' or skip to 'Old King Cole'. Rock and sway to 'Rock-a-bye baby'. Posters with the words should be included, and you can refer to these to comment on appropriate print features. This allows you to demonstrate important aspects of print such as:

- the difference between print and illustration,
- print is read from left to right,
- the consistency of similar words and letters,
- sound/symbol relationships through initial sounds.

Some teachers have found that an apron with large pockets which contain sets of props for different nursery rhymes is an attraction for children and helps focus their attention on the meaning of the rhyme and provides enjoyable opportunities for role play for multiple retellings. Pockets might contain for example:

Miss Muffett and her spider, a tuffet, and a bowl.
Little Jack Horner and his bowl and a plum.
A cat, a fiddle, a cow, a moon, a dog, a dish and a spoon.

Nursery rhymes and older children

Older children will also benefit from the rhythms and sounds and regular patterns of nursery rhymes. They can then make use of the patterns to write their own versions. This is a popular writing experience as it is simple, but children who are gaining confidence can also have a great deal of fun innovating to devise humorous texts such as:

> Hic, hic, dot, dot,
> The mouse fell in the pot.
> The pot was frying,
> The mouse was crying,
> 'Hic, hic, dot, dot!'

Share some of the poems in Quentin Blake's *Nursery Rhyme Book* or *Custard the Dragon and the Wendigo* by Ogden Nash with older children to set a light-hearted mood. Then invite the children to innovate on these rhymes, keeping the language patterns. First, you might need to brainstorm descriptions of 'monster parts of the body':

> *The* balaroo,
> *The* balaroo,
> *Its* nose *is* thick *and* azure blue!
> *Its* breath *is* foul *and* smells like hell!
> *Its* eye *is* red *and* tends to swell!

Or you might prepare skeleton texts of some nursery rhymes in the way that has been suggested in chapter 3, page 26. These frameworks can be used to give children the confidence to try writing their own, while highlighting the patterns of the language.

> As I was going to St Clair's
> I met a man with seven ____.
> Each ____ had seven ____,
> Each ____ had seven ____.
> ____, ____, ____, ____.
> How many were going to St Clair's?

This example taken from 'As I was going to St Ives' cannot fail to have rhyme and rhythm as long as the children rhyme the second verse with 'Clair's', and follow the poem's pattern precisely. They are always amazed with the end result. When children have arrived at an awareness of rhyme and rhythm, they are usually keen to try out their knowledge, and writing experiences such as the above allow them to do this. Of course, the end result must make sense, and to achieve this the children must make appropriate choices from the language options that are available to use. The children can compile class or individual books of their rewritten rhymes to share. These make very popular reading material.

Rhymes and rhyming stories

Poems that lend themselves to innovation have powerful learning potential for awakening readers and writers:

> Mother horse, mother horse,
> Always busy,
> Why don't you stop and play.
> No, I must find hay
> For my baby foal,
> He's been neighing for food
> All day.

Children must use words appropriate to the context to complete verses based on the language patterns. Obviously, if they choose to write about a mother duck, then they'll have to write about hunting for worms to feed a baby duckling who's been quacking for food. The children can brainstorm this kind of information first:

Animal	*Baby*	*Food*	*Noise*
duck	duckling	worms	quack
cow	calf	hay	moo

> Mother ____, Mother ____,
> Always busy,
> Why don't you stop and play.
> No, I must find ____
> For my baby ____,
> He's been ____ing for food
> All day.

Very simple rhyming stories have much to offer awakening readers and writers. *Danger* by Joy Cowley, a good example of one of these stories, can be added to:

> Look out for wagons,
> They are full of ____

Or *Poor old Polly* by Melser and Cowley can be rewritten:

> Old Polly found a ____,
> She swapped it for a boat.
> The boat wouldn't ____,
> She swapped it for a veil.

The position of the blanks in the poems is different and serves different purposes. In *Danger*, the children have the rhyme as a cue prior to filling in the missing word. In *Poor old Polly* they have to read on before they are able to predict what might be a valid choice for the deletion.

You can help children who are having difficulty finding appropriate rhyming words by suggesting that they work through the alphabet making a list of rhyming words. For example, using *Ten Loopy Caterpillars* by Joy Cowley, children can innovate:

> Ten loopy caterpillars
> Wriggling in a line
> One tied itself in knots
> And then there were nine.

You can help by reading the original verse with the children, and working out which words need to rhyme. Here you would highlight 'nine', and highlight the position where the rhyming word would occur. Next, suggest that the children make a list of words that rhyme with nine:

> dine
> fine
> line
> mine

The children might choose to write:

> Ten loopy caterpillars
> Going out to dine
> One jumped in the soup
> And then there were nine.

The list of rhyming words can be saved for future reference.

Other books to share and to use in this way if you wish would be *See You Later Alligator* by Malcolm Carrick and Peter Charlton. If the children were to innovate on this book, you could highlight the wonderful illustrations and perhaps make a class big book or a wall chart. To prepare for writing, you could have the children clap out the rhythm and note the number of syllables required for the person or animal being addressed: al–li–ga–tor, San–ta Claus, swim–ming fish.

Mary Ann Hoberman's 'Backward Town' (included in *Gobble Gobble Glup Glup* by Parkes and Smith) is an excellent poem to innovate on:

> The folk who live in Backward Town
> Are inside out and upside down.
> They wear their _____ inside their _____
> And _____ beneath their _____.
> They only eat _____
> And _____.

Shel Silverstein has written many poems in *Where the Sidewalk Ends* that children will love and which will give them ideas for writing. For example, 'Drats':

> Can anyone lend me
> Two eighty-pound rats?
> I want to get rid of my house of cats.

might become:

> Can anyone lend me
> Two eighty-pound frogs?
> I want to get rid of my yard of dogs.

Another excellent collection is Spike Milligan's *Unspun Socks from a Chicken's Laundry*.

CHAPTER 4

Encouraging independence

The needs of more independent readers and writers

By more independent readers and writers we mean those students who are aware of the role of literacy in their lives. They are aware that the written language that arises from and/or is part of a social situation will have purpose and meaning within that situation: e.g. reading a timetable to find out when to expect the next bus, reading an interesting book, or writing a letter.

Such children will need your help to explore other ways in which literacy is used because the forms of literacy (such as the structure or organization of text, grammatical structures, punctuation and print formats as well as other text features) vary with the situation in which they are used. Children need to be confident that they know what to expect in the text and can even begin to question information that does not seem to 'fit' because it does not fit with their own experience and knowledge. They need to be encouraged to become familiar with a wide variety of different types of texts.

They will also be willing to try to read and write more independently of their teacher because they have learned some of the strategies which readers and writers use. They will be matching to some extent the author's actual text as they read. They will also probably be moving towards conventions such as organization of ideas, grammar, letter formation, spelling, punctuation and so on, when they write.

However, independence and confidence in reading and writing usually emerge when situations and texts have become familiar. Learners may still falter in an unfamiliar situation dealing with previously unmet ideas, structure or language. So the strategies readers and writers use in different situations and the conventional forms of reading and writing must still be demonstrated and shared in your classroom. Important aspects of your programme will therefore include reading and writing to them and with them, as well as inviting them to be more independent.

These readers therefore need to discover:

- the expanded opportunities for enjoyment and learning that are available through reading and writing.
- the ways in which literacy is used in a wide variety of situations.
- the strategies that experienced readers and writers use in such situations to help them if difficulties arise as they read and write.

One child who is moving in this direction is Peter whose journey towards becoming a reader and writer is described in chapter 6.

Observing more independent readers and writers

Teachers therefore need to develop ways of observing developing literacy learners. They need to extend the scope of their observations to ensure they are aware of how adequately such learners are coping in new situations and with varied texts. They need to observe literacy in use in realistic situations.

The observations suggested in chapter 2 for looking at awakening literacy users are also valuable for more independent literacy users and others are suggested here. Others are outlined in a booklet published by TAWL (1984).

Observational technique 1

What aspects of language and strategies are readers using?

At times teachers will want to explore whether children are using effective strategies as they read but it is important to do so in as informal a way as possible. The teacher might, for example, invite children to share their favourite part of a text they are reading. As they do so, the teacher will, of course, be noting their responses to the text and also the reasons why they find the text interesting. This provides an opportunity to note their choices of books, and the teacher may wish at another time to suggest other books and topics that the children might read to extend their horizons as readers.

The teacher has an opportunity, as the children read aloud, to observe what these learners do when their responses are different from the text. For example, if a child is reading *Cinderella* and, instead of reading 'slipper', reads the word as 'slither', then the teacher will know that the child has lost the thread of meaning. It is necessary to decide the effects of such alterations (or miscues as they are called) on the total meaning. The teacher will want to think about whether the child's miscue responses:

- materially change the meaning, and therefore the cohesiveness with ideas earlier in the text: it is unlikely that Cinderella lost her slither.

- distort the grammatical structures: to read the word 'slither' instead of 'slipper' in the sentence 'Cinderella's slipper fell off' certainly leads to an inappropriate use of language.

The teacher will also want to note the strategies or steps the child takes if the alterations do create problems in meaning and grammatical structure. Generally if readers do experience problems they have several choices:

- They can read on, and this is a sensible choice if the meaning change is slight or the difficulty is related to something relatively unimportant in the total context.
- They can also read on for a while to see if there is further information which helps them sort out their thinking. They might also check print features such as headings and italics for the information these might provide. They could also make use of non-print information such as *illustrations*, *diagrams* and *figures* to see if these will help. As they do so, they will be looking for additional information to sort out the discrepancy.
- They may need to reread and see if they have omitted something that might help them.
- Sometimes they may decide to focus on that part of the text alone and check out the graphophonic features of the word. If readers continue misreading the same word, it is worth asking them at the finish of the reading what the word means. They may understand its meaning, even if they don't know how to pronounce it.

If children continually baulk at words or seem to be losing track of meaning in terms of what they have read previously, then it may be appropriate to tape-record their reading so that you have the opportunity to analyse the language features and strategies they are using. The teacher may wish to make use of the comprehensive analysis outlined in the reading-miscue-inventory procedures (Goodman, Watson and Burke 1987).

An interesting example of one child who is beginning to use a variety of language resources and strategies is included in chapter 6. James, as you will note, is moving from being a non-reader who confuses word and sound identification with reading, to becoming a much more independent, strategic reader. A recent sample of his reading is included in chapter 6, together with a commentary on his growing insights as a reader. By contrast, Peter, another child who is introduced in chapter 6, is an almost independent reader and, because he is so capable of dealing with miscues that would otherwise lead to an incoherent reading of text, there is little that is worth commenting on, beyond his strengths as a reader. He is using the strategies outlined above and making effective use of all aspects of language.

You will also find the reading development continuum developed by Chapman (1987), a useful model through which to investigate children's miscues. These may be collected during oral reading or through examining the replacements children make in completing cloze activities, or while innovating on text (see chapter 3, page 26). Chapman suggests that variations can be explored by considering the extent of the context and text which readers take account of in making miscues. He identified a continuum through which readers move in their awareness of the totality or cohesion of text and the related context. He identifies:

- the omission of words or giving of completely unacceptable responses, i.e. those which are totally outside the context, a response used by very inexperienced readers. In this case it is also necessary to question whether the reader has sufficient prior knowledge to make any connections with the text. Such a reader would be the one discussed previously who replaced Cinderella's slipper with 'slither'.
- the use of miscues and replacements which are only appropriate in the immediately surrounding text within the clause level by readers who are developing some awareness of text and relating it to a context. An example of this is a child who ignores the punctuation to read:

  He sat in the seat. At the front of the screen the cowboy rode on his horse.

as

  He sat in the seat at the front. Of the screen the cowboy rode on his horse.

to the point where readers who are moving towards effective reading as their responses show that:

- they perceive the clause structure but create errors in the overall meaning. Such readers do not recognize the subtleties of what the author is attempting to do. Or they may provide a response which is cohesive in the sense that it creates a text for them, but which is different from what the author intended. Such a reader might replace 'The clock struck twelve' with 'The clock stopped ticking' in the following passage:

  Cinderella danced with the prince until midnight. When the clock struck twelve she ran out of the room, and her slipper fell from her foot.

You will find it helpful to refer to Chapman's book, *Reading: From 5–11 Years* for a more complete discussion of this important area.

Observational technique 2

What do readers understand about what they read?

As well as the story-telling task discussed in chapter 2, teachers might also observe children as they discuss books they have read with their friends. If discussion circles (see chapter 5, page 60) are established in the classroom, these can provide a focus for observations too. Literacy circles are described comprehensively by

Harste and Short (1988) as part of the 'authoring cycle'. The book, *Creating Classrooms for Authors* is one you might wish to consult for this as well as for many other useful strategies for helping your students.

The focus for observations during classroom and group discussions will be on the ways in which the children relate the context in the book to experiences in other books, to other experiences in their own personal lives, or to contexts they have experienced through films, television and other media. It is the links they are establishing as they compare, contrast, and question the context of the story that you will be noting. The concern is not whether their interpretation is in some sense 'correct', but that they are creating links with their prior experiences and with those of their friends.

Other opportunities to observe learners' responses to what they read arise as they transform their experiences from reading books through:

- writing.
- art.
- role play and drama.
- doing things outlined in a procedural text such as cooking, craft activities, science experiments and so on.

The teacher will, of course, be observing how effectively the children are making use of the links between their knowledge and what they learn as they read.

Observational technique 3

What do writers know about writing?

Allowing reluctant writers to draft and rewrite their drafts prior to publication (Calkins 1986; Graves in Walshe 1981; and Hill 1984) provides opportunities for them to produce writing of which they can be proud. This approach provides teachers with many opportunities for informal observation of children's growing insights as writers. It also removes much of the stress experienced by reluctant writers when faced with one-draft writing.

Through exploring students' drafts and final work, teachers can evaluate the extent to which they use:

- the structure or organization that is appropriate for sequencing the type of text children are writing.
- the scope of ideas and related vocabulary relating to the ideas in their text which in turn allows writers to create a cohesive text.
- their ability to express their ideas appropriately and so demonstrate a growing awareness of themselves as writers and their readers as audience.
- grammatical structures that are appropriate for their purposes in writing and the audience they are writing for.
- spelling, print formats and other features of text.

In your evaluation you will, of course, be guided by what it is the students are trying to achieve as writers – their purposes and their intended audience.

Peter, the child who has been referred to earlier as a relatively independent reader, is still receiving additional help with spelling. He does not yet have sufficient command of spelling conventions to satisfy what he would like to be able to do as a writer. As noted in chapter 6, he is not willing to take risks and still has to explore a wide variety of graphophonic patterns as he spells, so that he may become a confident, risk-taking writer. At present his unwillingness to attempt to spell the words he wants to use limits what he can write.

CHAPTER 5

Helping readers and writers to become independent

Using community literacy resources

Most older children understand why people read community texts such as television timetables, advertisements and bus timetables. One of the most powerful ways of demonstrating to older reluctant readers and writers the importance of literacy can therefore be through the use of resources like these which are derived from events in our daily lives. This section suggests some ways in which teachers can involve their students in investigating some forms of community literacy.

Using newspapers

Every day children see adults reading newspapers for a variety of reasons, so they readily recognize newspapers as valuable and functional. The daily newspaper is therefore a useful resource for children who need to be encouraged to read. You could invite your students to write and produce a newspaper. They will become interested in the project once they realize the scope of what a newspaper contains.

It is helpful to have sufficient copies of the same issue of a popular newspaper to allow each child easy access to it. One with a magazine is particularly useful as it provides a range of options for children to select from – film and TV reviews, reports on new cars, cartoons and so on.

In one classroom we invited the children to survey a newspaper and, as we did so, they expressed an interest in different aspects of the paper. They soon began to recognize the potential for newspaper articles in school events which interested them personally. For example, dissatisfaction with the tuck-shop menu led to the inclusion of a survey form in the children's paper to collect the opinions of other children in the school about the lack of chips on the menu! Again, one boy's wish to advertise his surf-board for sale led to a section of classified advertisements. A space-factual story that children had written, based on a mock-up picture of a spacecraft landing in the school grounds, became the focus for the headline story.

Getting started

You might introduce the children to the newspaper by surveying and listing the features as the children identify them:

	Features
Page 1	Headlines, news story, index
Page 2	TV-programme review, TV and radio guide
Page 3	Weather

and so on through to

Pages 23/24	Full-page advertisements
25	Sports reports and scores

You might share the lead story and explore how the news is presented. Usually there is a brief summary of the major features of the story in the first paragraph, a number of subheadings introduce each section of the text, and perhaps there are also some photographs or other illustrations. After reading the first paragraph, invite the children to speculate on what the subheadings indicate the rest of the story might be about. Have them jot down their ideas.

When you all have finished reading the article, discuss whether the headlines, subheadings and illustrations were helpful. Then, with the children, go through the article and identify how the information is presented. Usually after the beginning synopsis there is some comment from people interviewed by the reporter, and then the events are presented in a time sequence. The article usually concludes with some comment about the actual or presumed outcome. The children can work out suitable headings, and a summary sentence about each.

What happened.
What people said.
Events.
What might happen next.

Invite each child, either individually or with a friend, to write at least one news article. Their choices can obviously be very varied, as they might write about current news that they have seen on television, school sports news, fashion articles, or really anything that interests them. Other popular topics include profiles of local dignitaries, perhaps the headmaster, reviews of favourite television shows, reports on class outings, and interviews with visitors.

When the children have decided upon their topics, you might help them brainstorm ideas and list these into a logical sequence such as the one outlined above. Then invite the children to browse through the paper, reading items of interest, and, after consulting the survey list, to select which other features they wish to write.

The development of the newspaper will, of course, provide a focus for writing-process approaches; and children can work together to edit and proofread the completed articles prior to publication. You might invite children to use a computer with word-processing software. Newspaper writing provides an excellent focus for introducing this type of software, as children act as reporters, editors and proofreaders.

It is important to keep publication date on target, and not to let it drag on. Children should have to meet deadlines, so times for editorial conferences need to be arranged. This might also be an opportunity to explore the personal use of timetables with the children. They might use the format employed in the newspaper for advising on TV programme times to set up schedules for each article, with times for reporters and editors to get together.

	Reporter	*Article*	*Editors*
Monday 1.30	Sue	Volcanic eruption	James and Dianne
2.00	James	World Cup	Sue and George

Sufficient copies should be published to enable your children to receive comments and feedback from their families and friends.

Many teachers find the response of children to newspaper writing, because of its relevance and audience, is such that it is a monthly feature of their classroom programme.

Using magazines

There is a wide variety of magazines on the market which deal with special interests – sport, make-up and clothes, television and video programmes, computers and motor-bikes – the list is almost endless.

Some of your children might be interested in publishing such a magazine, or at least in reading those which are related to their interests and, doubtless, represent areas in which they are knowledgeable. These should not be overlooked as a resource for involving reluctant and inexperienced readers.

One useful publication in Australia is *What's your hobby?*, prepared by Edel Wignell, which, as its title suggests, deals with hobbies such as collecting, pets, sports, card games, arts and crafts and so on. An interesting feature of this little book is that each section has a contribution by children written about areas in which they have a personal interest. It serves as an interesting resource, as well as a useful model for writing for hobby clubs or special interest groups. There are many others of the same type available in newsagents.

Using comics and cartoons

Most children love comics and cartoons as popular media forms such as these satisfy their need for fun and fantasy. Many of us will recall that Superman and Mickey Mouse were important to us when we were beginning to read! We found our comics enjoyable and read them regularly, and in that way became very familiar with the characters and the kinds of things they were likely to do and say. We also gained a rich experience of story structures from Mickey and Superman. As well, we learned about the print formats which are characteristic of comics, such as the use of speech bubbles, the extravagant use of punctuation marks and variation in print size and form to respond to what is happening in the story.

Share your favourite comic strips with your children so that they can see that you enjoy them. Invite them to bring their own favourites from family newspapers and magazines to share with everyone. Your children might enjoy making scrapbooks and posters, or keeping a constant supply of funnies on the noticeboard for everybody's amusement and regular sharing.

Learning about cartoon characters

Cartoon characters are well-known to children, and their predictable behaviour is the source of much humour. Garfield the cat is always lazy, greedy and mean-spirited. Charlie Brown of *Peanuts* is a born loser and Lucy is bossy, egocentric and full of her own importance. You could draw up a literary sociogram of the *Peanuts* main characters with the children's help and highlight how characters feel about one another. This idea is among many useful strategies suggested by Johnson and Louise (1985).

Of course, in developing such a sociogram children should give their reasons why they think Charlie Brown feels this way about others, and share incidents from cartoon strips to support their view.

You might suggest that children select one favourite character and write any words, phrases or sentences that seem appropriate to describe that character. They can share their ideas with the whole class or group, and invite others to guess which characters they are describing.

Next you could invite the children to write and illustrate little cartoon books that repeat and elaborate upon an idea:

> Charlie Brown should not trust Lucy *because* she always grabs the football.
> Charlie Brown should not trust Lucy *because* she teases him.
> Lucy should give up chasing Schroeder *because* he hates her.

Children enjoy writing and publishing small books such as this, with one page text, one page illustration. The books can then form part of the class library and are a valuable resource of predictable books for older reluctant readers (or anyone else).

Garfield is another antisocial character whom children enjoy writing about. You may wish to make use of Garfield cartoon books which are readily available. Older children love to read these, and to write and illustrate their own versions such as:

> You know you're having a bad day *when* you take off your coat and
>   realize you're still wearing your pyjamas.
> I'll go to the zoo with you *if* you promise to get into the monkeys' cage.

Take advantage of the opportunities provided by different cartoonists to invite discussion on features of comics and cartoons. For example, you and the children might discuss how the feelings of Garfield are captured in the pictures, and how the cartoonist uses brief speech and single words to capture the action that is going on. You can then use the class collection of cartoons as a resource, and invite each student to select a cartoon and write about what is happening in the chosen item. Children enjoy matching each other's written accounts with the comic strips.

Invite the children to produce their own cartoons, either by creating their own characters and situations or by using familiar comic-strip characters in their typical situations. To write their own versions, the children might like to use correction fluid to wipe out the text of a cartoon and write their own dialogue. Or they might draw their own illustrations and write original text. Another suggestion would be to combine characters from different comic strips so that for example 'Snoopy meets Garfield'. After experiences such as these, the children have an awareness of characters and strong story structures, and the role that illustrations play in building the cartoon's story.

Using jokes and riddles

Children enjoy and want to share jokes and riddles as soon as they are conscious of puns. There are many books of jokes and riddles available and the children's section of most newspapers and magazines also offer a wealth of reading material in these genres. You can all enjoy reading and writing knock-knock jokes, limericks, puns, riddles, hink-pink riddles, and so on.

Of course, you will need to demonstrate how each genre works prior to inviting the children to write their own.

Knock-knock jokes   To compose a knock-knock joke, the children will need to know the pattern:

> Knock-knock!
> Who's there?
> Teresa.
> Teresa who?
> Teresa green.

and then you might provide this skeleton text for them to use for innovation.

Knock-knock!
Who's there?
_____.
_____ who?
_____ (and the joke).

Also they need to think of a name which sounds reasonable by itself, but which can be used in a completely different way by adding further text, for example:

Who's there?
Ida.
Ida who?
Ida come if you'd asked me!

This is not easy for children to do so you might need to collaborate with them, perhaps making lists of names and potential endings. This might take some time, but the children will be delighted with their completed jokes. A collection of these jokes makes a very popular reading resource.

Puns and riddles   Children love riddles – they are always looking out for new ones so invitations to read and write them in school time are accepted joyfully.

You might spend some time with your children sharing riddles. One inviting resource is a book of riddles, *A Cat's Eye is One*, by Marcia Vaughan. In addition to providing a model for simple riddle writing, the transparent overlay sheet that comes with the book allows the answer to be seen when placed over the illustration. Some children might enjoy the challenge of creating a similar book.

Most riddles are based on puns and word play which seem to fascinate children. They prefer to read riddles rather than to try to write them, because riddles like this are not simple to compose: 'When is a new hat like an old one? When it is worn'. However you can provide the children with strategies to help them:

Suggest they think of words that sound exactly like others but which mean something quite different, for example, 'sea' and 'see'. Someone might think of 'horse' and 'hoarse'. Now suggest that they think of a question that could be sensibly answered by both words, for example:

QUESTION: Why is a pony like a person who has a sore throat?
ANSWER: Each of them is a little ho(a)rse.

Perhaps you could reserve a chart or blackboard for children to write their 'punny words' so they have a store in readiness for riddle-writing time.

Riddles could be recorded in books, displayed in the classroom or published in the class/school newspaper.

Other resources we have found to be useful are *Spooky Riddles* compiled by

Michael Dugan, *The Australian Children's Joke Book* by Heath and Ainslie Dillon, *The Animal Joke Book* compiled by John Allison.

Hink-pinks   These are rhyming riddles and are also very popular with children: 'What treasure did the pirate find buried in the iceberg? Cold gold and cool jewels.' In order to make a hink-pink, the children need to think of two rhyming words, usually an adjective qualifying a noun, e.g. 'sweet meat'. Once again the child has to devise a question that will be sensibly, but also amusingly, answered by the hink-pink: 'What would you call steak with sugar sprinkled on it? Sweet meat'.

Limericks   The rhythm and rhyme of limericks make them pleasant to hear and fun to read. These features make the genre considerably more difficult to create, so you could assist the children by initially providing them with models:

> There was an old lady from York
> Who loved roast potatoes and ＿＿ (pork, cork...)
> One night when she dined
> She swallowed some ＿＿ (find, rind...)
> And then ＿＿ it out with her ＿＿

Models, such as these with very few items missing, will give the children the opportunity to explore the rhyming words and rhythmic patterns they need to look for. When they are confident, you might move on to more open patterns and to inviting the children to try writing their own. The more banks of rhyming words they generate the easier this will be – and the greater the opportunity you will have to explore this dimension of language.

You can help them to use rhyme by highlighting the rhyming words that need to be replaced.

Extending the links between talking and writing

As was noted in chapter 3, language experience approaches help to make written language very predictable. The written language transforms what learners know and talk about into print. The strategies outlined in chapter 3 can be extended in several ways as learners become more confident as readers and writers.

You will have encouraged them to extend their awareness of how certain language patterns can be used and reused again and again. Now they can be encouraged to express their ideas more fully and make their writing more varied by adding elaborations in the form of adjectives and adverbs, phrases and clauses.

So as you and the students share writing in class reports and small group writing about classroom experiences, and as you respond to the children's drafts, you can discuss ways in which their original ideas might be extended.

For instance, as you and the children investigate plant growth in the ways outlined in chapter 3, the record of plant growth outlined there might be extended from:

It's got roots,
It's growing bigger,
Now it's got a shoot,
And now it's got a leaf.

to become:

OUR CLASS PLANT

We're growing a broad bean plant in a jar.
It's got a big root.
Every day it's growing bigger
and now it's got a large green shoot.

You might begin by inviting the children to suggest ways of making the title specific so that a reader would have more information about the text. They might suggest that 'broad bean' or 'class' would help, and the new title can be selected by them.

You might also discuss whether other people need to know more about where the plant is growing and this leads to the setting statement 'We're growing a broad bean plant in a jar', and to more information about the appearance of the plant – all of which leads to the meaningful introduction of adjectives, phrases, and so on.

Another important aspect that arises is the opportunity to discuss how we indicate in text the sequence of the events. The use of temporal conjunctions such as 'every day' or 'and now' is introduced in ways which relate to situations the children have actually experienced. If you or the children have kept a chart of the plant growth, this will be a very useful reference to use to introduce such a time sequence.

However, learners do need time and a variety of experiences so that they may become more confident in their ability as writers. You are probably at this stage still helping them to overcome a great reluctance to write, stemming from many experiences of what they – and others – have considered failures in the past.

Exploring literature in the classroom: encouraging independence

It is crucial that we include regular sessions of story reading in our programmes, to provide poor and reluctant readers with opportunities to enjoy the literature that other children who are effective readers enjoy as part of their own personal reading. Reluctant readers should not be penalized because they find reading difficult. They need to be invited into the world of books because this will be an incentive to them to keep on learning to read. Ineffective and reluctant readers still enjoy a story, if their television viewing habits are any indication. So they need to be kept aware that the world of books offers equal promise.

There is another very vital reason why we should include story reading as part of our programme. This is to ensure that underconfident readers learn about the nature of stories. A notion of 'storiness' will allow them to know what to expect in stories and so provide them with much more confidence as readers. Readers who are independent have developed this sense of purpose – of being in control, of having an idea of what will happen next when they read. They are aware, at least at a subconscious level, of the elements of storiness such as likely plot and types of characters. This provides them with the confidence to read, even though at times something in the plot, the language or even in the print may cause them to question the message they think the writer is communicating.

We can share the recurring features and variations provided through experiences with:

- different versions of the same story, for example the multiple versions of 'The little red hen'.
- common plots so, for instance, those who are rejected through the events of the story find new acceptance as in *The Musicians of Bremen* and *The Little Crayfish*.
- similar or the same characters such as stories in which children come to know about Paddington Bear, or Luke Skywalker, the children of Narnia; Dr Who became the focus of one child's initial exploration of stories for a period of a year!
- similar settings – stories that happen in space or in circuses, in the neighbourhood, or in a castle.
- the same author so that children might discuss some of the stories told by Roald Dahl.

Linking story plots

Story episodes have underlying motifs (Huck *et al.* 1987). The conflicts and their solutions depend upon such motifs as:

- magical spells and objects such as in *Cinderella*.
- taking journeys, a motif explored on page 30 of chapter 3.
- finding a home: a common motif of stories for younger children that underlies such stories as the adventures of 'The three little pigs'.
- finding oneself – an important issue for older children.

Getting started

Different versions of the same story: sharing different versions of the same story can be a useful way to begin. For instance, *The Great Big Enormous Turnip*, originally by Leo Tolstoy, is available in a number of versions. The plot is the same in *The Great Big Enormous Watermelon*, by Brenda Parkes and Judith Smith, except that the turnip becomes a watermelon and the characters who are involved in the latter version differ. Old Mother Hubbard becomes the watermelon grower, and she is helped by various nursery-rhyme characters.

Having shared the traditional story with children you might then turn to the alternative retelling (*The Great Big Enormous Watermelon*) which uses repetitive grammatical structures (or language patterns). A split-page format uses illustrations which reveal cues to the identity of the next nursery-rhyme character to appear. For instance, the reader can see the pail before Jack and Jill appear on the next page. Because of their knowledge of the plot of the story, and after the experience of sharing the first few pages, the children have the satisfaction of being able to 'read' with you with a great deal of confidence and purpose, and they can confirm their hunches using limited print information.

Common features of plot

To encourage children to think about the common features of story plots, it might be helpful to select several stories which have common features. One example of this can be found in two stories which are based on how the noises which some animal characters make interfere with other characters. This leads to the crises which occur in the two plots. The stories are *Good-night, Owl!* by Pat Hutchins and *Trouble in the Ark* by Gerald Rose.

You might first share *Good-night, Owl!* with the children and discuss some of the noises that bothered Owl and how he resolved his predicament.

After reading *Good-night, Owl!* to and with the children, you can investigate the plot. The children will enjoy suggesting other animals, people or things that might disturb him:

> donkeys bray,
> horses neigh,
> parrots chatter,
> monkeys chatter.

You might use the text and prepare a skeleton framework (see chapter 3, page 26) so the children can substitute other animals who bother Owl or other characters such as story or nursery-rhyme characters:

> The Little Dog laughs.
> Little Boy Blue blows his horn.
> The black sheep baas.

Then invite them to develop and illustrate their own new versions:

> The Little Dog laughed, hah-hah,
> hah-hah, hah-hah,
> The black sheep baa-ed, baa-baa,
> baa-baa, baa-baa.

———

The plot in Rose's book, *Trouble in the Ark* is essentially the same as that of *Good-night, Owl!* Problems are created for the main characters because of the noisy animals. Unlike Pat Hutchins, Rose uses the cumulative repetitive structure of 'I know an old lady' to tell his story:

> It was the fly who started the trouble.
> He buzzed mouse
> who squeaked at rabbit...

So after sharing this book and involving children in the reading, you'll probably find they may have a variety of suggestions about other stories they remember that are like this one. The plot may remind them of *Good-night, Owl!* or they may recall a cumulative repetitive story. Be very accepting of their ideas, as it is the links *they* establish with what happens and the characters involved in stories that help them develop a sense of storiness.

Your children might also enjoy creating, through shared and personal writing, some further 'trouble in the ark' in the form of other nuisances who trouble Noah and his wife. Or they may enjoy role-playing what happened as you reread the story.

Young children will enjoy reading *The Farm Concert* by Joy Cowley which is a book they will probably be able to manage independently after their previous experiences with similar books such as *Good-night, Owl!* by Pat Hutchins and *Trouble in the Ark* by Gerald Rose.

Again teachers should look for books which provide a common feature in the events. For example, the feature shared by the stories, *The Musicians of Bremen* retold by Brenda Parkes and Judith Smith, *The Bunyip of Berkley Creek* by Jennie Wagner and *The Ugly Duckling* retold by Brenda Parkes and Judith Smith, is that the events in the stories occur because the characters in all three stories feel rejected.

Taking the three stories mentioned as a model, a teacher might introduce the experience by reading a book such as *The Bunyip of Berkley Creek* or *The Ugly Duckling* or another book with a similar theme to the children. The bunyip is rejected by all the animals until he finds other bunyips, while the ugly duckling is similarly rejected by the other ducklings.

After the reading children can be invited to revisit the story. Reread the story and identify the story chain:

Kangaroo tats at dingo

Chris's writing, Trouble in the Ark *(a)*

The Bunyip felt sad when...
The Bunyip felt even sadder when...
The Bunyip felt even unhappier when...

When you have shared *The Ugly Duckling* you might develop a similar story chain. The children could compare the events which upset the two characters, and then how the two characters ultimately resolve their dilemmas when they find other animals who are like themselves. Of course, there is the interesting difference, that, whereas the duckling becomes beautiful, the bunyip does not change but is accepted for what he is.

mosquito bust kangaroo

Chris's writing, Trouble in the Ark *(b)*

Now through the reading and discussion about the dilemmas happening to some of the story characters you have set the scene. You might introduce the children to the independent reading of *The Musicians of Bremen* by first sharing with them the story of *The Little Crayfish* by Ursula and Celestino Piatti. Both stories deal with characters who are rejected, the crayfish because it wants to be different, and the musicians because they are too old to work. In both cases the characters join with others who resemble them to find a solution to their problems. The common features that *The Little Crayfish* shares with *The Musicians of Bremen* provide a good basis for children's predictions for the latter.

The version of *The Musicians of Bremen* by Brenda Parkes and Judith Smith is suggested for encouraging independent reading by children because it has been retold in a way that emphasizes the repetition in the plot through repetition of

his master talking to his wife.

His master said, "That donkey is getting old. Soon he'll not be able to work, so I'm going to get rid of him."

"Yes," replied the wife, "get rid of him. We don't want useless animals here."

The donkey was very sad. "I'll have to run away," he said to himself. "I can still bray. I'll go to Bremen and become a musician." So that night he ran away.

The donkey had not gone very far when he met an old dog limping down the road.

"Hello, dog," said the donkey. "Why are you out so late on the road?"

The Musicians of Bremen

language, and this is reinforced through the use of coloured print, using a print format as a cue that reinforces the repetitive aspects of the text. So after reading the setting and the first episode in which the dog and the donkey join forces, you and the children can share the illustrations throughout the remainder of the book, discussing your ideas of what might happen.

The children then, either individually or in pairs, should be encouraged to read the story, predicting what they don't know and making a note of anything that still puzzles them or anything that is of particular interest. They can discuss this with you and the other children at some point during or when they have finished reading the book. But it is important to encourage them to be as independent as possible: they must learn to take a chance.

When everyone has finished reading the story, involve them in a discussion of other stories or events they know which were like this one. Some might, for instance, recall the stories you have shared previously, perhaps *The Ugly Duckling* and its rejection, others might think of *The Little Tin Soldier*. Others might think of something that they have heard on television and so on.

Extending the experience

Because of the limited number of characters in *The Musicians of Bremen* it lends itself very well to a communal reading. You might take the part of the storyteller and the children could read the language spoken by the characters.

If you wish to revisit the common points in language between stories and everyday dialogue, the story of *The Musicians of Bremen* might be rewritten as a play. This might be a valuable experience for your learners, as the experience will involve decisions about how much of the story information needs to be rewritten as dialogue, and how much can be conveyed through the actions of the actors, or perhaps by having a storyteller. For example, the story opens:

> There once was a donkey who lived on a farm with his master. Every day for many years the donkey worked hard pulling the plough, carting wood and carrying heavy loads.

The children might write suitable dialogue for the donkey, or a storyteller could be used to relate this aspect of the story. However, the decisions that need to be made to provide the donkey with suitable dialogue would be valuable in encouraging the children to consider the feelings of the donkey. Would the donkey say, 'I'm sick and tired of working for my master'? Or would he say, 'I don't mind how hard I work. I want to please my master'?

The final text might be something like this:

> *Setting: curtain opens to show a donkey working hard pulling a heavy load. Donkey stops.*
> DONKEY: Every day I work and work. I feel so tired but I want to please my master.
>   I must get back to work...

The children might speculate on why such formats are used for presenting plays such as the identification of settings, stage directions, and dialogue: again this emphasizes the reasons why language changes in different texts, in predictable ways. It helps children understand that language is not random.

The children might also look for different ways in which direct speech is shown in written language. They could compare the way it is written in stories with the way it is shown in plays and also in cartoons. You might invite them to think about the reasons why these variations in print formats are used, and how the differences suit the purpose for which the different types of texts are created. For example, the children might realize that the illustrations are the most important feature of cartoons, and the speech can easily be indicated by the balloon format, while in a play it is important for the actors to be able to see at a glance when it is time for them to speak again, so the characters' names are highlighted.

You might also involve your children in other stories in which the characters are presented through the same theme. *Wilfrid Gordon McDonald Partridge* by Mem Fox for instance tells how Miss Cooper finds happiness when Wilfrid comes to her aid, or in *Crow Boy* by Taro Yashima which is about a boy who has been rejected by his classmates but eventually comes to be accepted by them. These are books which would be suitable for sharing and discussion by older children, and would be suitable independent reading for some.

After a number of children have read the stories, have them compare the ways in which the different characters find solutions for their problems. Their discoveries might be kept as an ongoing chart in your classroom.

STORIES THAT HAVE HAPPY ENDINGS		
Musicians of Bremen	The animals get rid of the robbers who are bothering the people	The ending was different than we expected.
Wilfrid Gordon McDonald Partridge	Miss Cooper gets her memory back when Wilfrid helps her	Miss Cooper reminds Susan of her grandma.

If the books suggested are not available you would, of course, find many others in your library, as this plight is a common one in stories.

You will, of course, want to allow for the in-depth investigation of other common plot lines by sharing the common features in such genres as adventure stories, mystery stories, historical novels, human-problem stories, friendship stories, myths and legends, and so on, as readers show their interest in such topics.

Linking story characters

Story characters are often larger than life and often represent human characteristics such as virtue, beauty, truth and evil. In traditional stories these characteristics are often matched by physical appearance, for example, a story might have a beautiful princess or an ugly troll. Some common representatives of evil in traditional stories are the giant (greedy and bullying), the fox (sly and deceitful), the witch (the embodiment of evil), and the dragon (who brings death and destruction). There are also stories where the giant or the dragon is helpful and is the hero. However, to appreciate this switch readers first must read with the expectation that giants are the representatives of evil. Similarly, other characters are traditionally 'good' or heroes.

Children who have read and enjoyed stories are aware of the different story characters. This makes a powerful source of prediction that they can use as a basis for one of their strategies when responding to stories. Poor readers who lack this experience need to acquire this sensitivity to story characters. It is therefore vital that teachers continue to invite their pupils to share exciting, well-written stories and experiences that highlight aspects of story characters.

Doubtless you have many favourites that you share with your pupils. As you share such stories with them, you will have opportunities to stop and have them speculate on what will happen next, based on their knowledge of other characters in other stories. Children should also be invited to discuss what they liked and did not like about characters in a story. Did they think the character acted the way they thought he or she might? What else might the character have done?

You will also want to follow up a story reading at times by inviting children to create their own sketches of characters as they imagine they would be, or to draw an illustration from an episode of a story which captures best the way they think about a character. Role plays and story writing are also powerful ways of inviting children to think about characters. They might write a diary of the day in the life of Alexander perhaps when he is not having such a terrible day (Viorst, *Alexander and the Terrible, Horrible, No Good, Very Bad Day*) or a new adventure for Brenda Parkes's McBungle as he sets out to search in the United States or England for a suitable pet based on *McBungle's African Safari* (Parkes).

Getting started: for younger children and even some older ones

It is helpful to find several books with story characters who resemble each other in some ways. One such pair is *The Hungry Giant* and *The Giant Jam Sandwich*. *The Hungry Giant* by Joyce Cowley has as its villain the giant who terrorizes the villagers in his search for food. Similarly, *The Giant Jam Sandwich* by John Lord has as its villain four million wasps who spread terror around them until ultimately outwitted by the villagers. These wasps may well remind the children of the very hungry giant. Both are overwhelmed by the villagers who ultimately seek their revenge.

The Hungry Giant by Joy Cowley is a very useful resource for young children because of its repetitive plot as well as its strongly written villain, the giant. The giant here is obviously mean as well as hungry, and after sharing the first few pages you will find most children will join in the reading with vigour and enjoyment.

Child's writing about giants

After one or two shared readings of this story, using the types of demonstrations we have suggested in chapter 3, children might enjoy writing their own version based on their knowledge of story characters. They could select an alternative villain, perhaps a wolf or a dragon, and write a new story version to share with their friends. For instance, the big bad wolf might decide he wants to eat a pork roast dinner and the trimmings: 'I want some potatoes', growled the wolf. 'Get me some potatoes or I'll blow your house down.' He might then demand beans and finally pork. He might suffer a terrible shock when the villagers, after searching for some time, produce a huge, savage wild boar.

Some children may need help in thinking through suitable collections of food that are likely to be found in one meal. A brainstorming session in which they are encouraged to think of such foods will help to get them started:

bread   butter   honey
chips   vinegar   fish
spaghetti   cheese   meat
cereal   fruit   milk

Perhaps the children might enjoy following through the theme of punishing the demanding character by finally producing the food source rather than the food, as happened when the villagers produced the beehive instead of honey. To do this they would need to plan their meal with this added dimension – as was done in all of the meals above. They could make a list of ferocious food possibilities, for example:

meat	bull, crocodile, bear, lion
fish	shark, giant squid
milk, cheese	cow, goat

Similarly, other related sets of objects, such as clothing, could form the basis for other stories, or sporting objects, such as cricket ball, stumps and bat, might also be used, depending upon the characters in the story.

You and the children might then read a book such as *The Giant Jam Sandwich*, and by now your children should be in a position to speculate on the fate of the wasps from very early in the reading. The children are likely to make very confident predictions on what will happen, based on their growing knowledge of the ways other villains are defeated.

Doubtless you and the children will have other favourite stories that you can share together as a basis for discussing the characters who live in stories.

For older readers

The Hobyahs by Brenda Parkes and Judith Smith is a book which features very strong descriptions of characters, particularly of the Hobyahs themselves. The book provides an excellent opportunity for revisiting story characters with older reluctant readers.

As you share this book with children, use an appropriate intonation pattern to mark the 'creepy ideas'. These are supported by the use of language and by the alliteration. Reread the book inviting the children to join you. This book, which is available in a big-book format, lends itself to repeated readings, with children joining in with suitably 'creepy' voices and actions, or perhaps tapping out the rhythmic patterns.

Creep, creep, creeping
On their toes and their knees
came the slimy, slippery Hobyahs.

To focus upon the characterization of the Hobyahs, you might invite the children to brainstorm other ways they could describe these rather unsavoury characters.

As they came, they whispered,
"Tear down the house, Heh! Heh! Heh!
Tie up the old man, Heh! Heh! Heh!
Tie up the old woman, Heh! Heh! Heh!
Then we'll put the little girl
in our Hobyah machine."

The Hobyahs

Hobyahs are		
grasping	repulsive	scarey
greedy	revolting	scrawny

Then, with your help they can innovate on the text changing the refrains to suit their ideas.

> Grasp, grasp, grasping
> with their long pointy paws
> came the ghastly greedy Hobyahs.

They might enjoy moving on to creating new characters, such as 'Gloppy floppy slopyahs' or 'Lanky lolloping limpyahs'.

Books such as *The Lorax*, a Dr Seuss book, and *The Twits* by Roald Dahl would make excellent resources for extending older children's knowledge of characterization.

Keeping a 'character register'

When you and your pupils are exploring a number of similar stories, for example, fairytales, or detective stories, one idea which highlights the predictability of story character types is a character register. This is a book or large sheet of paper which has designated spaces for character types, and into which new names are entered, as the children discover other suitable characters in the book that you are sharing or they are reading individually.

FAIRYTALE CHARACTER REGISTER

CHARACTER TYPES	STORIES	
	Cinderella	*Rumpelstiltskin*
Young, beautiful princess/girl	Cinderella	Miller's daughter
Young, handsome prince/man	Prince	King
Evil magic character		Rumpelstiltskin
Good magic character	Fairy godmother	
Evil villain		
Poor but honest character		Messenger

To have a character 'registered' a child could fill out a nomination form naming the character, the book the character comes from, the suggested character classification and some evidence to support the nomination:

Name of person making nomination _____

Name of book _____

Name of character _____

Character type _____

Reasons for this nomination

(1) Describe the character

_____

_____

_____

_____

(2) Why you are nominating the character

_____

_____

_____

_____

_____

The children will soon see just how common character types are in books of a similar type. They will enjoy opportunities to learn about filling in forms, revisiting stories and reflecting on story episodes to justify the decisions they made when categorizing the characters. This kind of language experience can be particularly non-threatening to inexperienced readers and writers, as they are free to make use of the story texts for most of their responses; so they are, in effect, using a print model in a very meaningful and purposeful way.

Extending character concepts

To extend the concepts of story characters and story plots further you might share Roald Dahl's *Revolting Rhymes* with your children; comparing his whimsical switches in character and plot with those in the more traditional versions of the tales. You might, for example, begin by sharing the reading and retelling of the story of Cinderella and then with the children's help list information about the plot and characters.

Then share the Dahl version of *Cinderella* together, and invite the children to reread this new version, with your help if necessary, and as they do so, compare this with the more traditional tale:

What happened to Cinderella	*What happened to Cinderella (Roald Dahl)*
Cinderella was not allowed to go to the prince's ball with her sisters. She was very sad.	Cinderella was not allowed to go to the prince's ball with her step-sisters. She got really mad.
Her fairy godmother gave her a beautiful ball gown and slippers, and lent her a golden coach.	Her fairy godmother gave her a beautiful ball gown and waved her wand. Cindy was at the ball.
About the characters	*About the characters*
Cinderella is sweet and kind. She loves the prince.	Cindy is bad tempered and scared of the prince.
The prince is handsome, kind, very patient.	The prince is cruel. He tears Cindy's clothes.

You and the children might then collaborate and write new versions of other tales. They might like to rewrite *Jack and the Beanstalk* or *Snow White* or one of the other stories that Dahl has recreated in his book, so that later they can compare their versions with his.

Discuss the original story, and then invite the children to suggest new personalities for the characters. You could encourage discussion to decide whether these suggested personalities are likely to contribute to an amusing new version of the plot. To assist this discussion you might keep a record of their recollections of the original tale and brainstorming:

Jack and the Beanstalk	*Our new characters*
Jack and his mother live in a mansion near a bean plant.	Jack is handsome and kind, but his mother is a witch.
They have a beautiful golden hen and it lays golden eggs every day.	She wants to make a spell and needs golden eggs and a crown.

The final drafts, duly illustrated, will provide the children with proof that they too can write and create something other people will enjoy. And they will have learned a lot about stories.

Story characters like me

You might also read more factual stories and invite children to think about the characters in these. For example, you might share *Alexander and the Terrible, Horrible, No Good, Very Bad Day* (by Judy Viorst) with the children. Then have the children list some of the terrible things that happened to Alexander.

Alexander did not like Monday because:

> He had gum in his hair.
> He dropped his sweater in the sink.
> He didn't find a car kit in his cereal.

Invite the children to tell about similar 'disasters' in their own lives and list these:
Frances did not like Friday because:

> She lost her hair band.
> She missed the bus...

Then invite them to write their own 'very good' or 'very bad' days, using the book as a resource for ideas and language.

A further extension

Janet and Allan Ahlberg's book *The Jolly Postman* is another outstanding resource to use as a basis for discussing story characters, and the relationships they have with one another and also the way that the language used by characters to communicate with each other serves to cue in the reader to these relationships. The Ahlbergs' book consists of the mail delivered by the postman to various well-known story characters, so that:

> Goldilocks sends a letter of apology to the bears.
> The wicked witch receives an advertisement for 'witch specials'.
> The wolf receives a solicitor's letter telling him to vacate grandma's house.

In other words, there are models for a broad range of text types: stories, greeting cards, letters, postcards which, because they are spoofs based on stories that everyone knows, provide enjoyable resources for reading and writing for reluctant learners.

Before sharing the story, you might keep a note of the types of mail that arrive in your letterbox for a few days. Bring the envelopes and any non-personal items along to share. These can then be listed on a large sheet of paper with the items you have brought attached alongside. You might note for example that you received:

1 letter
1 account
2 advertisements
1 magazine

To enhance the children's notions of the purposes for writing and the audiences to whom mail is addressed you might then extend your list to include such information as:

Correspondence	Who from	Purpose
1 letter	a friend	keeping in touch
1 account	a store	wanting money
2 leaflet advertisements	local shops	advertising their special offers
1 magazine	a publisher	discussing the news

Share your list with your children and invite them to survey the mail that arrives through their letterboxes at home. Ask them to bring a list of the types of mail they receive. They might also bring to school the unsolicited mail that their families have received and do not want.

Then share *The Jolly Postman* and, as you come to each mail delivery, invite the children to speculate on what mail might be sent to each story character. A letter for Goldilocks: it is probable it will be from the bears. What would they write about?

Similarly, what type of mail would the witch who lives in Gingerbread Bungalow receive? An invitation to a witches' meeting, an account for ingredients for making gingerbread, and many other possibilities arise. Your children will no doubt be delighted by the advertisements for frog powder, the wizard, and so on.

When you have read the book, the children might spend some time talking about favourite story characters and the types of writing they might do:

Cinderella	A letter of thanks to her fairy godmother
The little tailor	A wedding invitation
Puss in boots	A description of his travels to London for a magazine
The Hobyahs	A 'missing person' poster for the little girl

You will want to develop several of these ideas as models through shared writing. This provides an excellent opportunity to discuss ways in which the characters would write to one another. How would Cinderella feel about her godmother, and how would she write to her? You might look at the letters included in *The Jolly Postman* and see how each of these vary. The children could compare the letters written by Goldilocks with that from the solicitor, Mr Meeny, to Mr Wolf. They might find differences such as:

- Mr Meeny typed his letter, while Goldilocks printed hers.
- Mr Meeny's letter has an address. Goldilocks' has not. Why not?
- Goldilocks uses 'everyday language' compared with Mr Meeny who writes 'We are writing to you'. Invite your children to speculate on why he would say 'we' instead of 'I'. Can they think of anybody to whom they would write using language of that type?

- Goldilocks finishes up with 'love from' while Mr Meeny writes 'Yours sincerely'. How do your children finish off letters to friends? Would they ever write a letter using other endings?

Have a collection of traditional tales available from which your children can select. Make sure your favourite versions are available. Using these as a resource, the children could write appropriate correspondence using *The Jolly Postman* as a model.

When they are ready to share their drafts with others, have the children spend a little time on thinking about the ways in which language is used, depending on how well the characters know one another and the relationships of the characters. Have them revisit the types of language people use to one another when writing.

They might also think about the ways in which they are going to prepare their final copies – typed, handwritten, special print – and also look carefully at the different formats used in the correspondence and on envelopes in the Ahlbergs' book. For example, why does the occupier have to 'Open now – don't delay'?

Linking ideas across contexts

Children need to be encouraged during reading to relate ideas to their own personal experiences and to the more vicarious knowledge they have gained through watching films, listening to story telling, enjoying role play and other games, and so on. Authors invite their readers to create such links through their choice of language, the use of illustrations and other forms of non-print information.

Authors also make use of synonyms, antonyms, and superordinates (more generalized terms used to refer to something which has occurred earlier in the text, so that 'tins' and 'crates' may be referred to as 'containers') to create links within their texts. Such links between ideas also help readers build bridges to their out-of-book experiences. They may not always know the meaning of a word but may infer it when the writer uses another word to refer to the same or related idea. Collocation, or words that commonly relate to a common context, such as sea–sand–waves–gulls, also help to create these textual and contextual links.

Metaphor and similes are other important ways through which language is used to create textual and contextual links. Writers may say, for example, a glove is a house for a hand or a throat is a house for a hum, inviting their readers to use alternative contexts to create an enriched context for the text. The use of metaphor can also be extended so that the reader links not only glove–house–hand but may move on to link sock–house–foot. As well as linking envelope–house–letter the reader can immediately see other relationships such as that letters enter an envelope through the 'door' and then the door (flap) is shut.

Getting started

A House is a House for Me by Mary Ann Hoberman is a delightful book which invites readers to look about and discover a world full of metaphors about 'containers'. It demonstrates how easy it is to find things that are containers or are contained. It provides an excellent resource for introducing inexperienced readers to some of the ways writers create a wholeness (or cohesion) in text.

Initially the container concepts are linked to human shelters, 'A hill is a house for an ant ...', but, as the text progresses, the ideas become more abstract and expand to invite readers to think about houses in a way they probably have never considered before: 'My head is a house for a secret ...', to 'The earth is a house for us all!'

Sharing the text

After sharing the book involve the children in thinking about some of the following questions:

What is this book about?
What is the most interesting idea?
What is very different?
Is it a story?

If the children discuss these issues in small groups, they will have more opportunity to put their own individual views. Have them record their responses for sharing and comparing with everyone later. Have them discuss what they think a house is now they have read the book. Invite the children to search through the text for examples of different kinds of houses. They can then decide how houses might be classified. Their classifications might include:

natural houses for animals.
human-built animal houses.
houses for machinery.

When the children have identified some different 'house' categories, they could look for other types and find related examples in the book. They might think of other examples that are not in the book.

They can then select one category and list examples. They might like to cut out a suitable card outline which matches their category so that they might represent houses for machinery by making a garage shape. They can then record the examples they found in the book, together with any others they think of that will fit on to their card shape. They will enjoy sharing their ideas, and the reasons they selected the examples they did, with other children. The shapes can be used to form a wall display for all to enjoy.

By now most children will be ready to write their own 'house' metaphors.

You could collaborate with the children to create one or two examples. Then invite them to write their own house metaphors to compile into a class book or group book.

Some children, however, might still be confused about the difference between 'container' and being 'contained', and so might write something like: 'A root is a house for the ground'. You can help a child who responds this way by revisiting less abstract examples like 'a web is a house for a spider'. Then discuss which is the house and which lives in the house. Again an example like 'cartons are houses for crackers' can be used to sort out which is the container and which is housed in the container. The children can then collaborate in small groups to write a page for a class 'A house is a house' book.

Child's version of A House is a House

Demonstrate how you would write one page and the children will be more confident when you ask them to try a page of their own. If they are having difficulties innovating on the text, suggest they begin by using small cards and blu-tack to cover the part of the text they wish to change. Then they need to write only those words they choose to fill in the blanks. When each page is completed, the authors can write out their final drafts and illustrate them. The book should be provided with an appropriate cover and be bound, before joining your class library.

Spelling

This might be the point to introduce children to a 'Slick Brick Wall'. Set aside a display board and invite them to help you to prepare the cardboard cutout 'bricks'. Tell them that the cardboard bricks are intended for the wall, but to be useful on the wall they must feature a pair of rhyming words. The book *A House is a House for Me* is particularly useful as it contains so many rhyming words, many of which are used as alternate graphic patterns, for example, 'hutches' and 'duchess'. Invite the children to write on the cards any appropriate words they find in the text. This is a useful demonstration of the visual patterns in spelling.

The slick brick wall can be an ongoing activity in your classroom. After its initial introduction the children can add to it and create a store of jokes, cartoons and riddles using the rhyming words.

Moving on

Now most of the children will be ready to begin making use of other metaphors. It is important that they see how this form of reference is used in literature all the time. You could introduce them to a number of poems that are presented as extended metaphors, starting perhaps with 'A Modern Dragon' by Rowena Bastin Bennett.

Share and discuss 'A Modern Dragon' and invite the children to identify the ways in which the author is comparing a train to a dragon. Have the children identify the ways in which this happens:

> a train is a dragon
> a train roars like a dragon
> a train wriggles like a dragon's tail

and so on.

They should have opportunities to share a number of examples over a period of time. Other poems which are helpful can be found in *Poems and Verses* (Childcraft 1974) and include:

> 'Palace' by Dorothy Vena Johnson.
> 'Garment' by Langston Hughes.
> 'Brooms' by Dorothy Aldis.
> 'Fog' by Carl Sandburg.
> 'Clouds' by Christina Rossetti.

When the children have sampled a number of the poems, you could introduce a brainstorming session where they are invited to suggest ideas for metaphor making. You might like to begin with something like 'I'm so forgetful – my head is a sieve', and illustrate this by dressing up a sieve with your sunglasses and a headscarf. The children will enjoy this, and they will be quick to come up with other ideas like 'Your hair is a mop', or 'My head is a garden for my hair'.

They can illustrate their ideas by drawing, painting, modelling or any other appropriate form. A picture of a dragon wearing glasses and sitting at the teacher's desk, or a mop with a face can be mounted as a mobile to illustrate their ideas, and provide interesting ways through which children can explore the concept of metaphor.

If some children are finding metaphor-making difficult, you might invite them to think of something that they use often, such as their feet. Then ask what they do with their feet? Perhaps somebody might respond that feet are used for:

> walking around.
> running.
> sliding.
> etc.

You could choose one of these, for example, 'walking around', and say something like:

> People walk around on their feet.
> Cats walk around on their ____
> So paws are feet for cats.

or

> Cars get around on their wheels
> So we might say that wheels are feet for cars.
> This means that shoes for wheels would be ____?

This kind of discussion using metaphors about common things seems to help children to understand metaphor.

Children should be encouraged to explore metaphors in other content areas or fields. Perhaps they might explore consumption through the metaphor of food in the same way as container was explored through the metaphor of house. And the children might write a new book such as *Food is Food for Me*.

If the children decide on food then they will need to gather information about food. They might help you to grow some mushrooms or some other quick-growing plant that will be ready to eat within a few days. If, for example, mushrooms are the choice, you will need a mushroom kit or some mushroom compost and a box with plastic lining. If there are no instructions with the kit, then prepare some so that the children will have the opportunity to read and respond to another procedural text. The children will also enjoy cooking and eating their crop.

Exploring mushroom foodchains By this time the children have seen what mushrooms need by way of nourishment to grow. You might begin by inviting the children to talk about the mushroom dish that they have just eaten and ask them what made the mushrooms grow. Once they have established that mushrooms need rotting organic matter, they can then identify similar uses of different types of organic matter. All of this information can be shown on a diagram as links of a chain. This provides the opportunity to explore the idea of how living things are used by other living things: compost - mushroom - me.

Invite the children to discuss other food chains: grass–cow–milk–me; seed–hen–eggs–chicken–me.

You might also involve the children in discussing what they themselves need in order to grow, and so move on understanding the metaphor of how the food others eat becomes food for me.

You will now be ready to begin demonstrating food metaphors to the children. One way of helping them to make the necessary connections is to return to the 'house' categories already discussed and look for related 'food' metaphors:

Houses for machinery garage	*Food for machinery* petrol
Houses for ideas head	*Food for ideas* sights conversations sounds books

Now invite the children to think up categories of 'food users':

food for people,
food for animals,
food for plants,

and to extend beyond: in Hoberman's words to begin 'farfetching'. You could demonstrate by showing how the rain–cloud cycle can be written as a metaphor for food:

Rivers feed from the clouds.
Clouds feed from the sea.
The sea feeds from the rivers.

and so now to:

food for vehicles
food for clouds
food for the sea
food for writers
food for newspapers
food for computers
food for thought.

Working individually or in small groups the children can compose their own food metaphors such as animal/vegetable food chains or the chain suggested by the rain--cloud cycle.

'Our food is food' books   You might revisit *A House is a House for Me* before beginning to write the new book, *Food is Food for Me*. The language patterns in the original will provide a structure for the children to use in their writing. Also the children will need to be able to refer to the various metaphors they have created during their work on this context. When the books have been written and illustrated, they could be shared and celebrated.

Linking myths and legends

Myths and legends can be found in the literature of many cultures. One delightful tale is one from West Africa, which accounts for 'Why mosquitoes buzz in people's ears'. The version we found was retold, under that title, by Verna Aardema, with illustrations by Leo and Diane Dillon. This book makes an excellent resource for encouraging readers to move on to relative independence as readers and writers because, after the initial setting, the plot is both repetitive and cumulative. At the same time it has the characteristics of a legend because it explains why natural phenomena exist the way they are today through recounting fictional events in the past.

You might begin by revisiting with the children some of the types of experiences suggested in chapter 3, page 36, 'Linking conversation with the language of books'.

Getting started

Before reading the book *Why Mosquitoes Buzz in People's Ears* the students might like to make their own predictions about the problem posed by the story: why do mosquitoes buzz in people's ears? This provides experience for children in story structures which emphasize how problems are solved. You could list the children's predictions and invite them to add new predictions as you share the illustrations with them:

> Why mosquitoes buzz in people's ears:
> Because mosquitoes want to keep people awake
> Because the iguana would not talk to the mosquito

As you share the illustrations you might also discuss the names of various animals that are found in the jungle, such as antelopes, iguanas, and pythons, that may be unfamiliar to your students.

Now for the reading

You might share the reading of the story until you reach the meeting of the animals, because this sets the pattern for the rest of the story. Then invite the children to read the rest of the book by themselves, first drawing their attention to the pattern of the language:

> Did you hear?
> It was ...
> who alarmed the monkey
> who killed the owlet –
> and now Mother Owl won't wake the sun
> so that the day can come.

Encourage them to build upon the pattern of the story and the language.

After everyone has finished reading, have them think about other stories they have read that remind them of this one. They may recall stories about jungle animals, or they may remember other legends they have heard or read. Invite them to explain how the stories are alike.

A strategy for dealing with unusual words   This book has a number of words which your students may find unusual and somewhat unpredictable. Ask them to browse through and identify words they think look puzzling and then suggest what they think the meanings of such words might be. For example the author includes such phrases as 'sat down, pem, pem, pem, around a council fire' or 'King Lion pulled out the sticks, purup, purup'.

Invite the children in small groups to discuss how they interpreted such words. The range of ideas will probably be quite varied. Have them reread the relevant parts of the text and discuss how appropriate the suggestions seem to be, and why. They might, for instance, look at the sentence, 'He began screeching and leaping kili wili through the trees to warn the other animals'. What does 'kili wili' mean? They can reread the preceding paragraphs together, and this will help to make it clear that there was something dangerous in the forest. The children need to understand that this limits the possible range of meanings for 'kili wili'.

Revisiting the story   You or one of your better readers might take the part of the storyteller, and several children could represent the king at least for the refrains. Other children could explore the sound effects (purup, badamin) and be responsible for joining in with these appropriate.

Comparing how people say things   Another feature of this book which is worth exploring is the language used by the characters when they talk to one another. They speak very formally.

> KING LION: Mother Owl, why have you not called the sun? The night has lasted long, long, long, and everyone is worried.

Invite the children to rephrase the language as if they were speaking for someone who is not a king in a story. For example they might say:

> MOTHER: Owl, why didn't you call the sun? It's been dark for a long time, and we are all very worried.

The children too might discuss how they would say this if they were speaking to their friends. This will open out discussion on how we use different language depending upon who is talking and who is the audience.

Moving on

Have a good selection of myths and legends in the book corner, and invite children to read and compare some of these. Some children might also be interested in writing their own myths. Books such as *Where Does the Butterfly Go When It Rains?* by May Garelick and *Where Does the Sun Go at Night?* by Mirra Ginsburg, which were included in chapter 3, might provide simpler models for the less experienced readers and writers and would be suitable for innovation on text. Some children might enjoy extending the story of *Why Mosquitoes Buzz in People's Ears* by writing a further episode to the story.

Exploring literacy through the curriculum

Children are involved in using a wide range of different types of text as they move through different areas of curriculum. They have extensive opportunities to learn how and why literacy is useful. However the less able children have fewer opportunities to learn from reading and writing as they are frequently unable to read the written-language resources that are available. They miss out on opportunities to learn about the specific features of language as well as the potential learning opportunities available from reading and writing such texts. So inexperienced readers and writers face the double jeopardy of failure in school subjects and the loss of valuable opportunities to become more effective as readers and writers. We need to approach this problem in several ways.

First, we need to be sure that delays in literacy learning are not interpreted as a general inability to learn. An ineffective poor reader or writer is not *per se* unable to learn other things. There are other alternatives to print media which can be used in introducing them to new ideas. We need to be sure that such readers and writers have adequate knowledge of the content so that when they do come to read and write about the topic they can do so confidently. So we need to provide them with other opportunities to explore first some aspects of the context, such as direct experience, experiments, role play, films and other media, and so on.

Second, while teachers may be concerned mainly with the content of the curriculum, it is important that time is spent with poor readers and writers demonstrating features of the texts which are appropriate to the situation to which they relate. For instance, poor readers and writers need help in learning how to read science and social studies texts, and they will benefit from demonstrations of how to use features of such texts.

Again, teachers might share some of the more complex books, using the opportunity to demonstrate the strategies readers use when dealing with texts such as these, and to invite the children to reflect upon their own strategies. This is a technique suggested in unit 2 on page 95.

Several units of work are presented here which are built around aspects of the curriculum. The literacy resources suggested are ones we have found to be particularly helpful because they are about topics which are of general interest, and because they incorporate a variety of text structures. Moreover, the texts include graphic and print-format features that are characteristic of their genres. You might choose to use other topics and other books, but we hope the ideas included here will help you design experiences and incorporate the investigation of aspects of text which will clarify for your learners how literacy and language can help them to learn, read, and write more effectively.

Unit 1: Things that change in nature

One excellent resource is a procedural text entitled *How to Grow Crystals* by Honey Andersen. The topic of the book is self-explanatory and is one which appeals to children. The text consists of a series of experiments preceded by some helpful advice, a table of contents, a glossary, and information about where materials can be obtained. The book also explains how to make models of crystals. The experiments involve opportunities to:

- read and write making use of 'hands on' resources and some illustrations.
- compare crystals with non-crystals and different types of crystals with one another.
- record observations, with the book providing a resource to help with difficult words, layouts and so on.
- make three-dimensional models to compare with real-life objects.

Getting ready

Preparations for experiments will involve your children in the kinds of literacy tasks which we do every day, such as checking recipes and manuals to make sure all the equipment and materials needed are at hand. Individually or in small groups, the children can be responsible for listing the items needed and ensuring that if these are not available they are included on a shopping list.

MAKING YOUR OWN CRYSTALS

Comparing the results

1   Compare the size of a washing soda crystal to the size of an alum crystal.
   - Which crystal did you think would be bigger?
   - Were you right?
   - Where were there more crystals – on the cotton or on the side of the jar?
2   Now try the same experiment using salt or sugar. Try to guess how big the crystals will be and how long they will take to form.
3   Draw up a chart like this:

Crystals	Size of crystals	How long they took to grow
Alum		
Salt/Sugar		
Washing soda		

4   Compare the results of your experiments.

How to grow crystals

You and the children might share the reading of the first few pages of the book within the context of setting up and trying out the first one or two experiments. Then as a group you might develop a brief report on the outcome of the first experiment to accompany a display. If this is their first experience with writing texts which report on information, then the children will quite probably be unsure of the kinds of decisions writers need to make when writing such texts, so you might need to model some of the ways writers make decisions in such situations.

A text of this form needs to be appropriate to the situation (an experiment) and to the roles of the children in that situation (scientists). In other words the tenor of the language should reflect that of scientists reporting their findings and be objective and factual:

CRYSTALS AND NON-CRYSTALS

Crystals have flat surfaces and straight edges. Other materials are different and are therefore not crystals.

Salt and sugar have flat surfaces and straight edges, so they are crystals.

Tea leaves do not have flat surfaces and straight edges so they are *not* crystals.

So in developing such a text you and your children might need to discuss whether they will report about what 'I saw', or whether it should be about what 'we all saw' and can therefore be 'authorative' as in the example.

One helpful way to prepare for this discussion might be to encourage the children to keep notes of the observations they make throughout the experiments and then come together to see what each child observed: 'Bobby found that tea leaves had curly edges. Ruth said that salt was shiny and very flat.' And so on.

Because the structure of text is to be a comparison, you might then list examples which are crystals and those which are not, and include the reasons given for the categories selected. Then together you and the children can work out some generalizations that apply to crystals and non-crystals.

CRYSTALS	NOT CRYSTALS
have flat surfaces	do not have flat surfaces
have straight edges	have straight edges
Salt has flat surfaces	Tea has curly surfaces

In developing the text, children will also need to discuss the language of comparison, and so think about conjunctions and other words that can be used to contrast things. 'Salt has flat surfaces *but* tea does not.' '*While* sugar lumps have straight edges, a cornflake does *not*.'

This type of experience will ensure your children have adequate information about crystals and have used the related vocabulary. This will also familiarize them with the language and formats involved so that they can move on to reading and writing about crystals without your help.

The crystals they make, any models they develop, and their written reports should provide an interesting display for the school's library or some other public area, and the feedback to your children should provide them with the audience they need to encourage them to further efforts.

Extending the investigation

This theme might be extended in a variety of ways by your children, either individually or in pairs, investigating topics such as:

- changes in weather.
- chemical changes.
- physical changes resulting from the application of heat and cold.
- rainbows and colour changes.

They might enjoy preparing lists of directions for making instruments to measure changes in the weather, or instructions for conducting experiments, similar to those in the book they have been working from, *How to Grow Crystals*. These resources could be shared with one another and with other classes.

Unit 2: Processes

Processes that occur over a period of time or space are represented in language through the use of conjunctions and other words which reflect the organization of information in a time sequence. Authors and illustrators frequently support such texts with diagrams and models.

A book which provides opportunities to explore these dimensions is *On Site* written by John Pollock. This book is a factual book which outlines the various stages that are involved in planning and erecting a building. As well as clear line drawings, the book has a flow-chart and a glossary and is available both in large-book format as well as small individual books for children. The large-book format can be very helpful in class and group discussion on the graphic features in the text.

Getting ready

You might introduce this unit by investigating a shopping centre in your own neighbourhood to record the types of buildings, the types of businesses and their relative locations.

Such an excursion provides an opportunity to involve the children in preparing a permission form to allow them to leave the school grounds. You might discuss how such forms can be designed so that the same form is appropriate for everyone to use. This will lead to a discussion of the typical information and format of forms that are so common in our daily lives. They will realize that information such as name, address and telephone number is needed. Have the children identify the specific information that will be needed in relation to the planned class outing. They will need to think about the information their families will require and what type of permission you will need to receive back in turn.

The excursion Each student will need to take a pad and pencil for sketching and noting the types of business places they see. If you can photograph the buildings this would be particularly valuable for work when you return to the classroom.

If possible, try to include a visit to a building site, the theme of the book, as part of your excursion.

On your return to the classroom have the children categorize the types of businesses and see which might be interdependent, and therefore why they would be close together. Children might identify similar types of shops so that people shop for their food needs and so the butcher, supermarket and greengrocer might be close together. Or people often obtain medicine after visiting the doctor, so doctors' surgeries and chemist shops are close together. Children might work out other reasons for locations of businesses such as closeness to transport and car parks.

Food	Butcher	
	Greengrocer	} close to the car park
	Supermarket	

Health	Doctor	
	Dentist	} near a bus route
	Chemist	

Transport	Garage	} on a main road
	Tyre repair shop	

Again you might wish to take advantage of the opportunity to demonstrate the language used to talk and write cause-and-effect structures:

Our shopping centre
In our shopping centre, the doctor, the dentist and the chemist are all close together. This is very handy *because* if people go to the doctor and need medicine, they can get it from the chemist.

Different children can take responsibility for reporting on the part of the excursion they found most interesting as they write to such visitors.

If possible, invite a person involved in the building industry or a handyman to come to visit the class to talk about the work he or she is responsible for. You might use the opportunity to involve the children in the decisions writers make when writing letters of invitation.

Before your visitor comes you might share the illustrations in the book with the children and have them identify those which seem to provide information about your visitor's work. Then have them decide what subjects they would like to ask about, bearing in mind the occupation of your visitor. As an interview involves an interviewer and an interviewee, have them watch someone being interviewed on television, and make a note of the type of questions the interviewer asks. They can then frame some questions of their own. For example, if your visitor is an electrician, the children might want to ask:

What sort of work do you do mostly?
Which job is the most difficult?
Who do you have to help you?
What materials do you use? and so on.

Having a question to ask will help the shyest child to become involved.

Your visitor might also be willing to talk about other jobs involved in the building industry, and might also be able to provide the children with extra insights by discussing the big book illustrations with them. In particular he or she might talk to the children about the work done in some of the occupations shown on the flow-chart.

Later you might have your children reflect on the way the flow-chart illustrates the sequence in which buildings are erected. The value of flow-charts as a way of sequencing information is an issue that can be discussed.

Reading and writing with some independence

Before the children read the book, you might make a list of words you have specially selected from the text. Invite the children to look for these words in the glossary at the back and then to decide upon meanings for words they cannot find, before reading the text. They might also glance at the glossary to see what types of words are included.

	PREDICTING WORDS	
Word	*What I think it means now*	*What it means in the book*
permission (page 9)		
excavation (page 16)		
reinforcement (page 19)		
segments (page 22)		
technician (page 27)		

Some of the children may be able to read the book independently, but most will probably be pleased to read and discuss it in a small group situation. This can therefore be an opportunity to discuss strategies for dealing with unusual ideas and concepts, and the major purpose for using the book is to talk about books of this type; hence the value of the big-book format on this occasion.

You might, for instance, read the introduction and, when you have finished the page, ask the children if there is anything they do not understand. Discuss the ideas contained in the paragraph in relation to the illustration and to the experiences you have been sharing in the classroom. You might also ask them to predict what the major focus of the book will be – is it the idea of 'building activity' or of 'co-operation between people'? Their previous experience and survey of the pictures and diagrams will probably encourage them to select the latter theme.

Revisiting meaning After the students have finished the book you might together revisit the word-prediction lists and reread the pages from which the words were taken. Invite them to describe the meanings they would put to the words now they have read the text. Discuss with them whether they would change from their first prediction, or whether they are satisfied with the meaning they chose first.

You and the children might also create a flow-chart showing 'What happens when a building is developed' as the children finish reading each section of the book. This will involve deciding what information is relevant, and how some words provide a cue to the time sequence in which things happen. They might discuss what help words help them to decide the time structure of events – words such as 'when', 'eventually', 'next', 'then' and so on.

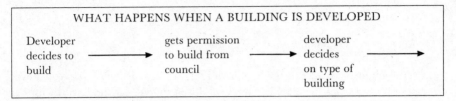

WHAT HAPPENS WHEN A BUILDING IS DEVELOPED

Developer decides to build ⟶ gets permission to build from council ⟶ developer decides on type of building ⟶

The children may also look very carefully at the diagrams in the book and decide what information can be obtained from them. They might compare, for instance, the difference between a quantity surveyor's estimate and a service plan, and decide why they are different. Some children will enjoy identifying what information they can discover by looking at the cross-section and longitudinal drawings included in the book.

Again the diagram illustrating the stages in erecting a crane is of interest. The children could compare the information in the written text with that available in the diagram, and list what they found out by reading the text and by looking at the details in the diagram. The two sets of information could be listed for comparison as a table showing 'What we read' and 'What we saw'.

Looking at glossaries   Have the children check out the glossary and compare the words there with the ones you talked about as you read. Have them reflect on whether this glossary is helpful. They might reflect on other words they would choose to include, and why.

Extending the investigation

Art and architecture   Children might enjoy exploring books such as *Cathedral: The Story of its Construction* by David Macaulay, a book which traces the building of medieval cathedrals in the same way as *The Site* discusses erecting modern buildings.

Craft   Some of the children might like to design their 'ideal' house. They can use the design of the building in the book *On Site* as a model for ideas for designing their floor plan, elevation and cross-section. They might enjoy illustrating the exterior of their house, and the layout for the different rooms. Some might enjoy planning a layout for telephones, electrical fittings and so on, which they can also base upon the plan in the book.

Choices which allow students to revisit the ideas underlying flow-charts could include:

• historical topics – such as the change in transport over the years – this could include a flow-chart.

- procedures – the steps involved in making something including diagrams. This could describe a craft that the children are interested in, or something they have seen being made.
- geographical themes – tracing the water cycle or the journey of a river.
- social change – how dress has changed over the years.

Unit 3: Characteristics and traits

Some factual books gain their predictability because they provide information about expected characteristics or attributes of the topic. This is very helpful when introducing learners to the attributive structure in text. So, when writing a book about people of a certain country, an author will fairly predictably write about the appearance, dress, food, housing, occupations, leisure, religious beliefs, and so on of the people. Or in discussing animal or botanical species, typically information will be organized around a discussion of the relationships amongst the members of the species: their appearance, location, food requirements and so on. In other words the organization of the text depends upon how information is structured in that field of knowledge.

It can therefore be helpful for developing readers to move from a study of human families to one of animal families, or to relate spatial characteristics of a topic in geography to those used in spatial mathematics. You may need to demonstrate to developing readers and writers how these characteristics help make written language predictable to readers, and help writers organize what they write.

Getting started

Because wildlife is a topic of widespread interest and generally familiar to children, this is a useful topic to introduce books organized through the attributes of this field. *The Platypus* by Joan Short and others is a useful book. If you think for a moment – what do you expect to find in a book of this type? Perhaps there will be information about the animal's habitat, its appearance, its diet, how it protects itself . . . In fact a check with the table of contents shows that the information is about physical features, habitat, food, reproduction, and protection of the animal. Experiences with this or other books, similar to those outlined below, help establish expectations about factual books. In introducing the book you might share the cover with your children. Invite discussion about what sort of book they think it will be – is it likely to be factual or a story? Why? Issues such as the title itself and the photographic illustrations would suggest it is factual. For instance, is the title referring to only one platypus – the one illustrated, or is the author indicating that it is a book about more than one platypus?

Contents

Contents page of The Platypus

You might also refer the children to the back cover where they will find information about the authors. It is interesting to find out why the authors wrote this book, and the information contained in the biographical details, such as the authors' occupations, suggests it is likely to be a factual book.

You might then have the children predict what will be in the book and then have them check their ideas with the table of contents. Together you might list the topics in the table of contents, and then, with your children looking only at the information here and on the front cover, see how much information (right and wrong) you can generate together about the platypus.

Feet – like a duck's.
Breathing – probably like a fish because it lives underwater.
Not like fish, it lives in a burrow.

The children in this way will be sharing their background information about the animal.

Now have the children survey the book, looking only at the major features of the book such as the importance of information revealed by print-format features such as size. Help them to list the illustrations and diagrams and talk about what they can discover from print-format features and other sources of non-print information. For example:

WHAT WE LEARNED FROM ILLUSTRATIONS AND DIAGRAMS

Platypus has webbed feet, short tail, fur, an ear which is a slot behind the ear, and a bill with nostrils along it.

Feet webbed for swimming. Webbing pulled in when it digs.

Male is about 500 millimetres long, and female is shorter (about 450 millimetres).

Also have them turn to the glossary and survey this for any term they do not know, or that they think they might need help with. Have them locate the item in the text.

By the time they have finished this survey, they will have very considerable knowledge about the platypus and therefore be able to make use of the links that the authors have created throughout the book e.g. the platypus has webbed feet, a bill, a furry body, and so on. This will help make the text predictable as they read it, because they will understand what the author is likely to say about the attributes of the body of a platypus.

Reading and writing with some independence

Many children might now be able to read from this book without further assistance. If some are very reluctant, a friend might share the reading with them.

Cloning an author

This is based on one of the many excellent strategies suggested by Harste and Short (1988). Have the children read one chapter and, as they do, note on a sheet of paper the four or five facts that they find the most interesting. For example, one child might select:

> webbing tucked in for digging.
> venom in spur behind legs.
> cannot breathe underwater.
> female lays eggs in nest.

When the children have finished, have them cut their paper into the separate sections, so that each fact is on a separate piece of paper. Then have them arrange their slips so that they put the slip with what they consider is the most important information in the centre, and place those that they think deal with related ideas together. One child might arrange his or her papers this way:

> [legs]
> webbing tucked in for digging
> venom in spur behind legs
>
> female lays eggs in nest
> [compared with say the kangaroo]
>
> cannot breathe underwater

Others will obviously have other ideas and sequences.

Invite the children in pairs or small groups to discuss the slips they have prepared and combine the slips, discarding any that are the same. Have them decide which is the most central information.

The children might then record 'Interesting information about the platypus' based on the central pool of ideas.

Extending the investigation

Other animals Experiences such as those outlined above, though perhaps appearing to be somewhat time consuming, are most important as they provide children with insights into the varied resources that readers and writers use to help them.

Children could be involved in the preparation of factual books which have a similar structure. Jim Howes's book, *Animal Jigsaws*, could be an excellent resource for developing readers as the text is simply written and contains information about a variety of animals.

First, you might survey the book together, looking at the variety of animals which are included. Basing their work on the previous discussion about animal attributes, children could select one animal and summarize the information provided. Have the children decide upon suitable headings around which information could be organized. Their experience with *The Platypus* will provide them with ideas as headings that might be used to identify animal characteristics.

For example, the information about the chimpanzee could be subdivided into much the same categories as those used in the table of contents in the book, *The Platypus*.

	THE CHIMPANZEE
Introduction	Chimpanzees are our closest relatives in the animal world. They look and behave like us.
Appearance	They are hairy and big....
Food	
Protection	

With this information and structure, a four- to six-page booklet could be written about chimpanzees, with appropriate topic headings, a table of contents and a glossary. Such books would be suitable for sharing with younger children, who would doubtless love to have a book written and read to them by an older child.

Plants Another useful investigation could be based on a book entitled *Five Trees* by Jim Howes. This book contains useful information about five different trees and uses a very appealing format to identify the uses of each tree. The big-book format in which this book is presented, in addition to the individual standard-sized format, provides a model for presentation of information in a way which we have found very useful for children who are still underconfident readers and writers. The uses of each tree are shown by the author and the illustrator through a large illustration with a brief statement about how each part of the tree is used by something else.

The children could prepare their illustrations on a large poster sheet as happens in *Five Trees*. They can then attach brief statements about the different aspects of the topic. This form of presentation allows the children to produce a final draft without too much difficulty because each task is broken down into small segments.

CHAPTER 6

An account of two children revisiting literacy

To illustrate issues raised about reluctant and inexperienced readers and writers in this book, the progress of two children is discussed below.

Moving towards independence

James is an eight-year-old who is rapidly becoming independent as a reader and writer. Until recently he thought reading was a question of identifying words and print, and so he was almost totally reliant on words he could recognize and his limited knowledge of print. While he enjoyed having stories read to him, and therefore must have had some awareness of the nature of stories, he appeared to ignore this knowledge when he was trying to read. He would substitute inappropriate words, guessing from phonic information alone, and then read on despite his obvious failure to make any kind of sense. However, more often he would sit quietly trying to fathom out individual words until he sought help from the teacher. When he was told the individual word that was bothering him, he made no attempt to reread or to fit this word into the context of the text. In other words, reading was a matter of recognizing a series of words, if possible. The outcome of all this was, of course, that James could not read even very simple texts and had no confidence in himself as a reader.

He has now had many experiences which have involved sharing predictable stories and stories that were of particular interest to him. He has had experiences with innovations on text which have shown him how text is a cohesive predictable whole. He has had many demonstrations that his own knowledge and information available in the illustrations can be used to predict meaning, and to help him confirm what he thinks the meanings print might be conveying. His teacher also shares the strategies she uses as a reader with him. Reading and writing have been closely interlinked in the ways suggested in chapter 3.

Now he is aware that print does present information with meaning, and his expectations about meaning become obvious when he repeatedly searches the text, the context and his prior knowledge. The following example of his reading of *Jack and the Beanstalk* by Judith Smith and Brenda Parkes will help illustrate his insights as a reader.

Attempt 1   The   opened one   there ext –
      2   These   only one   there ext –
      3   They   opened one
      4   There's   no one   here except me

There's no one   here except me
said the old woman.
So the Ogre sat down at the table
and the woman gave him some food.
Jack lay very very still in the oven.
                 fin (thin).
He was very very frightened.

Jack looked at the Ogre
Attempt 1   money.
      2   gold.
and he looked at the gold.
'That's my gold,' he thought.
Attempt 1   slowly
      2   slaughtered
'The Ogre sold my cow.'
So Jack crept out of the oven
and he grabbed the bag of gold.

You will notice in his efforts to read this extract he shows his determination to make sense of: ' "There's no one here, except me," said the old woman.' James first read this as: 'The opened one there ext...' and knew that made no sense. His use of phonic information represented an approximation as he was confusing the letter order, '*opened* one' and probably 'only' confused him. However, his willingness to try this was a marked advance on his earlier strategies as a reader when he either recognized a word or did not know what to do.

Next he tried: '"These only one there ext me," said the old woman.' He clearly showed that he knew that he was dealing with something that the old woman said, and obviously she must be talking to the giant, and not to Jack. So then he tried: 'They opened one...'

Then obviously the meaning, language and print came together at this point. He had some expectations of what the old woman might say to the giant, and he worked very hard at finding an option for 'There's no one' that would make sense. Perhaps he realized that this would be a sensible option, taking account of the semantic and grammatical information. Perhaps he also realized that 'one' which he had already noticed could be preceded by 'no', given the print information.

Again James read 'fin' for 'frightened', a seemingly incongruent miscue, unless his listener is aware that he always substitutes the sound 'f' for 'th' because of a minor articulation problem. So James was really thinking about how 'thin' (and not 'fin') Jack must have been, probably because he could fit in the oven. He was clearly aware of a suitable context and was attending to this as well as what he knew about print.

Another interesting miscue occurred when James read: ' "That's my gold," he thought. "The Ogre sold my cow." ' as ' "That's my gold," he thought. "The Ogre slowly...." ' ' ' "The Ogre slaughtered my cow." ' James has linked the context of the story with his past experience, as he lived in the country for some time and knows what happens to cattle that are sold for beef, i.e., cows that are sold get slaughtered. He used his phonic knowledge selectively in that he was aware of the 's' and the 'l', but he did not take account of the length of the word he used to replace 'sold'. However, he also recognized that the grammatical structures he had used were not appropriate once he had read on beyond the word 'slowly'. Clearly James is using much more effective strategies as a reader and attending to what he knows with far more confidence than previously.

The nature of the miscues and the self-corrections that James made while reading *Jack and the Beanstalk* show that now he is an intentional reader. He expects reading must make sense and knows that he needs to read further or to reread if the text he creates ceases to have meaning for him. He knows where to search for cues to create this meaning. His use of phonics, which was once his only resource, is proving to be insufficient to meet the demands of the reading materials he is now enjoying. No longer is he constrained to make do with restricted choices of words and ideas. He does, however, need further encouragement to write in order to learn more about print. A sample of writing by James is shown on page 108.

Sense of storiness

Evaluating this final draft we can see that James still needs to learn more about story structures. He had obviously intended to write a story about Redbeard but then moved to a story about Redbeard's crew. He showed his knowledge of story structures when he added the fierce storm and the rescue. He used a logical time sequence, but did not always use the appropriate temporal conjunctions or words that indicate the conflicts in the story.

Content

James is interested in pirate stories, and this is evident in his use of such vocabulary as 'fierce pirate' and 'fierce storm' which are appropriate to the content. However, he moves from one episode to the next without ever fully developing the ideas. This means that there is limited descriptive language. James

Once upon a time
lived Red berd a
fese pirat . his freinds
didint like Red berd
sowe thay were bad
to Red berd sowe thay
throwe Red berd over
borde . and the pirets
went to shore
and tund into kinde
pirets Now thay help
rete ships. and One day
a . fise stome kame and the
good pirts were in the stome
thay got stak on roks
the people thay saved save
the pirets

James's writing, 'Once upon a time'

may not yet have sufficient knowledge of the field to elaborate on his ideas. For example, he could not find a more effective way to describe the relationships between Redbeard and his so-called friends other than to say 'they were bad to Redbeard'.

Grammar

On the other hand James demonstrated an awareness of some of the grammatical patterns commonly used in stories when he wrote: 'Once upon a time lived Redbeard, a fierce pirate.' But his inexperience is again evident in his inappropriate use of nouns and pronouns. This is apparent when he wrote: 'His friends didn't like Redbeard so they were bad to Redbeard so they threw Redbeard overboard.'

Spelling

James is willing to use invented spelling which allows him to experiment with word patterns and gives him the freedom to express his ideas. This writing sample shows that he is comfortable with a wide range of letter sequences and that he mainly uses appropriate or nearly appropriate phonic alternatives when inventing his spelling. He is quite obviously attending to all parts of the phonological aspects of words when he writes 'didint' for 'didn't' and spells 'pirates' as either 'pirats' or 'pirets'. He is also overgeneralizing some patterns such as 'kinde' instead of 'kind' or 'stome' for 'storm'.

James has learned a great deal about spelling, but he obviously needs more reading and writing experience to continue his growth as a writer. He will also benefit from appropriate experiences that focus on specific letter patterns or print features which he knows he needs to learn about in order to move his own writing closer to conventional print.

A relatively independent reader and writer

Peter, prior to his present programme, was an underconfident eight-year-old who appeared to be terrified when asked to read or write, so much so that at first he even perspired when asked to read aloud. Peter's mother explained that he had missed some school in his first grade because of asthma and family upheaval, and that, although he always seemed to be trying to do what was required of him, he just could not cope with reading. When Peter was asked what good readers would do when they come across words they do not know, he suggested they would 'sound it out'. He said he enjoyed those occasions when his teacher read to the class.

Peter took some time to gain confidence in himself as a learner. His understanding of learning seemed to be that the teacher tells the children what to do and they learn this by rote. Beyond trying to meet this expectation, Peter appeared to have no personal purpose for learning to read or write. Perhaps the understandings he did have about the meaningful use of print, such as his self-confessed enjoyment of listening to teacher-read stories, were not connected to the 'activities' he associated with learning to read. It was difficult to help him to make this connection.

Peter was always a conscientious student. Once he understood something of the usefulness of literacy and learned some useful strategies, he became much more comfortable as a reader and a writer. Now, when Peter reads, he makes deliberate use of what he knows and does so slowly and systematically. He is quite unlike James who responds impulsively. Asked to choose a book to read, Peter first examined each front cover and read the back cover information, looked through the illustrations, and even read some of the text. Eventually he chose *Rumpelstiltskin*, retold by Edith Tarcov.

Attempt 1	all	
2	all over	
3	something	even
4	almost	evening

On the third day it was almost   evening
when the messenger came back.

'I could not find any new names for you,'
he said.
'Not any new names at all?'

'Well,' said the messenger. 'I did find

Attempt 1   strong
Paused, read on silently,
then self-corrected.
Attempt 2   strange

something. Something very strange...'
'Tell me,' said the queen. 'And hurry!'

So the messenger told the queen what he had found.

'Last night,' he said, 'I went up high,
high into the mountains.

Attempt 1   down
I went deep into the woods

**where the fox and the hare say good night
to each other. There I saw a little house.
In front of that little house there was a fire.
And around that little fire**

Attempt 1   far
repeated, then
self-corrected.
Attempt 2   fire
a tiny little man was dancing.

Peter read the story slowly, looking at each illustration before proceeding to read each page. He constantly sought information from the text and context by using strategies such as reading on, rereading, attending to useful phonic information and pausing to think about what would be sensible options. He was never satisfied to proceed unless he had created a cohesive text.

For example, when he was reading 'On the third day, it was almost evening...', these are the alternatives he explored:

On the third day, it was (pause) all...
On the third day, it was all – over...NO!
On the third day, it was (something) even when the
messenger
On the third day, it was almost evening
                                        evening when the
messenger came back.

He used his understanding of the context and his phonic knowledge to arrive at 'strange'. First of all he picked up the 'str–ng', and he knew that this sequence resembled 'strong'. His appreciation of what was happening in the story would not allow him to be satisfied with this option. He read a little further and looked at the illustrations while he thought about what else the word might be.

When Peter read 'down' for 'deep', this did not interfere with the meaning he was creating, so he did not correct it. However he did self-correct, using his knowledge of language patterns, to solve the problem he created when he read 'around that little *far*' instead of 'around that little *fire*'.

While Peter is willing after careful thought to take some risks as a reader, the kinds of strategies he uses as a writer show that he is not yet a risk taker as a writer. He tries to change his ideas so that his text includes only words that he can spell confidently. Quite obviously he still has a way to go as a speller.

The illustration on page 112 is an example of Peter's writing and demonstrates how he is becoming sensitive to many aspects of story writing.

baby blue berd   was   triying to fly
he   fell   done   from   her   tree
brok   her   Wing   she   was in pan
all   at   wones   she   saw   a   big.big   cat   she wa
afigd   as   she   tried   to   fly   away   but   she   cac
fly   she   saw   a   man   and   ran   strat
wordes   him   as   the   cat   was   strat
her   tayil   the   man   looked   at   the   berid
strugeling   to   get   away   from the   big   black
the   man   picked   the   blue   berid   and   ge
it   home   it   was   very   sike   wen   they   got h
man   was   going   to   operrat   him   self   but   he   said
it   kill   it   but   he   rang   the   vet   and   they
strat   away   and   they   operrated   on   her.

Peter's writing, 'A baby blue berd'

Storiness

Peter demonstrates that he has learned a great deal about the way in which a successful story is structured, developing effective episodes showing both conflict and resolution of the problem. He placed the baby blue bird in a dangerous situation, showed how the bird tried to get away from this situation, and then developed further suspense by making these attempts fail. Even when the bird was eventually rescued, its problems continued until finally a home visit from a vet resolved all. Peter would benefit from looking at how other authors create a more vivid setting for their stories before thrusting their characters into the conflict.

Vocabulary

While Peter has used a limited vocabulary to create his story, it is coherent, and he shows a sensitivity to the bird's dilemma.

Grammatical structures

Peter has made use of grammatical structure to enhance the suspense of his story, when for example he writes: 'The man looked at the bird struggling to get away from the big black cat.' Peter is omitting full stops, but he is separating his text very definitely into sentence units. Only his final sentence shows signs of his lapsing into a more immature style, with idea units joined by 'and'. Because Peter is still using 'and' and 'but' as the major conjunctions to link his ideas, his structures appear far less mature and effective than they are. He will benefit from reading and writing experiences which emphasize alternative ways of linking ideas in text.

Spelling

Peter's spelling of the words he uses most frequently is approaching the conventional form. While his other spelling shows that he is making some use of approximations, he does need to be encouraged to make more extensive use of this option. This would remove the restrictions he is placing on himself as an author and would provide further opportunities for him to investigate the patterns of letters involved in spelling.

By choosing, in collaboration with Peter, only a very limited number of visual patterns included in the writing sample, and discussing conventional ways of dealing with them, his teacher can, in fact, make him aware of some aspect of the conventional spelling of a much wider range of words. For example, if they were to choose to discuss 'brok', they could also discuss words with similar visual patterns such as:

choke
smoke
coke

or they could, as a spelling strategy, discuss the effect of final 'e' in such words as 'cane, kite, Pete, cube'. Information such as this is only useful to children when it is taught within a context where they have some need for it.

We hope this account of the journey of two children, together with the experiences we have suggested, will be of help to you as you continue your involvement with other children who are similar to James and Peter.

Teacher references

Baghban, M. (1984), *Our Daughter Learns to Read and Write*. Newark. International Reading Association.

Bissex, G. (1980), *Gnys at Wrk*. Cambridge. Harvard University Press.

Calkins, L. (1986), *The Art of Teaching Writing*. Portsmouth. Heinemann.

Cambourne, B. (1984), 'Language learning and literacy' in Butler, A. and Turbill, J., *Towards a Reading-writing Classroom*. Rozelle. Primary English Teachers Association.

Chapman, L.J. (1987), *Reading: From 5–11 Years*. Milton Keynes. Open University Press.

Goodman, Y., Watson, D. and Burke, C. (1987), *Reading Miscue Inventory: Alternative Procedures*. New York. Richard Owen.

Harste, J. and Short, K. (1988), *The Authoring Cycle at Work in Classrooms*. Portsmouth. Heinemann.

Harste, J. and Short, K. (1988). *Creating Classrooms for Authors*. Portsmouth. Heinemann.

Harste, J., Woodward, V. and Burke, C. (1984), *Language Stories and Literacy Lessons*. Portsmouth. Heinemann.

Hart, N. and Walker, R. (1977), *The Language of Children: A Key to Literacy*. Sydney. Addison Wesley.

Hart, N. and Walker, R. (1984), *Teacher's Book. Level 1: Mount Gravatt Developmental Language Program*. Melbourne. Longman.

Hill, K. (1984), *The writing process: One Writing Classroom*. Melbourne. Nelson.

Huck, C., Hepler, S. and Hickman, J. (1987, 4th ed), *Children's Literature in the Elementary School*. New York. Holt Rinehart and Winston.

Johnson, T. and Louise, D. (1985), *Literacy through Literature*. Melbourne. Nelson.

Tansley, P. and Panckhurst, J. (1981), *Children with Specific Learning Difficulties*. Windsor. NFER–Nelson.

TAWL (Tucsonians Applying Whole Language) (1984). *A Kid-watching Guide: Evaluation for Whole Language Classrooms*. Occasional Paper no. 9. Tucson. College of Education, University of Arizona.

Walshe, R. D. (ed.) (1981), *Donald Graves in Australia: Children Want to Write*. Rozelle. Primary English Teachers Association.

Resources for children

Anon. (1985), *I Know an Old Lady: A Traditional Story*. Melbourne. Ashton Scholastic.

Aardema, V. (1975), *Why Mosquitoes Buzz in People's Ears*. New York. Dial Press.

Ahlberg, J. and A. (1986), *The Jolly Postman*. London. Heinemann.

Allison, J. (ed.) (1987), *The Animal Joke Book*. Melbourne. Ashton Scholastic.

Andersen, H. (1986), *Breathing*. Melbourne. Ashton Scholastic.

Andersen, H. (1986), *How to Grow Crystals*. Melbourne. Ashton Scholastic.

Bayley, N. (1981), *Nicola Bayley's Book of Nursery Rhymes*. Harmondsworth. Puffin.

Bennett, R. B. (1974), 'A modern dragon', in *Childcraft. How and Why Library, Poems and Verses*. Chicago. Field Enterprises.

Blake, Q. (1983), *Nursery Rhyme Book*. London. Cape.

Bolton, F. and Snowball, D. (1986), *Growing Radishes and Carrots*. Melbourne. Ashton Scholastic.

Brown, M. W. (1951), *Fox Eyes*. London. Collins.

Carle, E. (1974), *The Very Hungry Caterpillar*. London. Hamish Hamilton.

Carle, E. (1975), *The Mixed-up Chameleon*, London. Hamish Hamilton.

Carrick, M. and Charlton, P. (1976), *See You Later Alligator*. London. Deutsch.

Childcraft the How and Why Library (1974), *Poems and Verses*. Chicago. Field Enterprises.

Cowley, J. (1980), *The Big Toe*. Melbourne. Rigby.

Cowley, J. (1980), *The Hungry Giant*. Melbourne. Rigby.

Cowley, J. (1982), *Danger*. Melbourne. Rigby.

Cowley, J. (1983), *Dan, the Flying Man*. Melbourne. Rigby.

Cowley, J. (1983), *The Farm Concert*. Melbourne. Rigby.

Cowley, J. (1983), *Who Will Be my Mother?* Melbourne. Rigby.

Cowley, J. (1985), *Ten Loopy Caterpillars*. Sydney. Advertizer Magazines.

Dahl, R. (1980), *The Twits*. London. Cape.

Dahl, R. (1984), *Revolting Rhymes*. Harmondsworth. Puffin.

de Paola, T. (1978), *Pancakes for Breakfast*. London. Voyager.

Dillon, H. and A. (1981), *The Australian Children's Joke Book*. London. Angus & Robertson.

Drew, D. (1987), *Animal Clues*. Melbourne. Nelson.

Drew, D. (1987), *Caterpillar Diary*. Melbourne. Nelson.

Drew, D. (1987), *The Life of the Butterfly*. Melbourne. Nelson.

Drew, D. (1987), *Tadpole Diary*. Melbourne. Nelson.

Dugan, M. (1978), *Dragon's Breath*. Harmondsworth. Puffin.

Dugan, M. (1987), *Spooky Riddles*. South Melbourne. Macmillan.
Elliott, J. (1982), *The Incompetent Dragon*. London. Scholastic.
Fox, M. (1984), *Wilfrid Gordon McDonald Partridge*. Adelaide. Omnibus.
Fox, M. (1986), *Hattie and the Fox*. Melbourne. Ashton Scholastic.
Garelick, M. (1961), *Where Does the Butterfly Go When It Rains?* London. Scholastic Books.
Ginsburg, M. (1981), *Where Does the Sun Go at Night?* London. Franklin Watts.
Gunson, J. (1985), *Mr Smudge's Thirsty Day*. Auckland. Reed Methuen.
Hoberman, M. A. (1982), *A House is a House for Me*. Harmondsworth. Penguin.
Howes, J. (1987), *Animal Jigsaws*. South Melbourne. Macmillan.
Howes, J. (1987), *Five Trees*. South Melbourne. Macmillan.
Hutchins, P. (1968), *Rosie's Walk*. Harmondsworth. Puffin.
Hutchins, P. (1975), *Good-night, Owl!* Harmondsworth. Puffin.
Ireson, B. (1970), *The Young Puffin Book of Verse*. Harmondsworth. Puffin.
Lord, J. (1972), *The Giant Jam Sandwich*. Boston. Houghton Mifflin.
Macaulay, D. (1974), *Cathedral: The Story of its Construction*. London. William Collins.
Melser, J. and Cowley, J. (1980), *In a Dark Dark Wood*. Melbourne. Rigby.
Melser, J. and Cowley, J. (1980), *Poor Old Polly*. Melbourne. Rigby.
Milligan, S. (1981), *Unspun Socks from a Chicken's Laundry*. Harmondsworth. Puffin.
Nash, D. (1977), *Custard the Dragon and the Wendigo*. London. Frederick Warne.
Parkes, B. (1987), *McBungle's African Safari*. Melbourne. Nelson.
Parkes, B. and Smith, J. (1984), *Gobble Gobble Glup Glup*. Melbourne. Nelson.
Parkes, B. and Smith, J. (1984), *The Ugly Duckling*. Melbourne. Nelson.
Parkes, B. and Smith, J. (1986), *The Great Big Enormous Watermelon*. Melbourne. Nelson.
Parkes, B. and Smith, J. (1987), *The Hobyahs*. Melbourne. Nelson.
Parkes, B. and Smith, J. (1987), *The Musicians of Bremen*. Melbourne. Nelson.
Piatti, U. and C. (1973), *The Little Crayfish*. London. Bodley Head.
Pollock, J. (1987), *On Site*. Melbourne. Ashton Scholastic.
Pollock, J. and Y. (1986), *Trucks*. Melbourne. Ashton Scholastic.
Rose, G. (1975), *Trouble in the Ark*. Harmondsworth. Penguin.
Seuss, Dr (1971), *The Lorax*. New York. Random House.
Short, J., Green, J. and Bird, B. (1987), *The Platypus*. Melbourne. Ashton Scholastic.
Silverstein, S. (1974), *Where the Sidewalk Ends*. New York. Harper and Row.
Smith, J. and Parkes, B. (1984), *Animal Mothers and Babies*. Melbourne. Nelson.
Smith, J. and Parkes, B. (1984), *Jack and the Beanstalk*. Melbourne. Nelson.
Smith, J. and Parkes, B. (1987), *Beginnings Poster Book*. Melbourne. Nelson.
Snowball, D. (1986), *Chickens*. Melbourne. Ashton Scholastic.
Tarcov, E. (1973), *Rumpelstiltskin*. New York. Scholastic.
Tolstoy, A. (1972), *The Great Big Enormous Turnip*. London. Pan.
Vaughan, M. (1986), *Tails*. Melbourne. Ashton Scholastic.
Vaughan, M. (1987), *A Cat's Eye is One, and Other Riddles*. Melbourne. Ashton Scholastic.
Viorst, J. (1972), *Alexander and the Terrible, Horrible, No Good, Very Bad Day*. New York. Atheneum.
Wagner, J. (1973), *The Bunyip of Berkley Creek*. London. Longman.
Wignell, E. (1987), *What's Your Hobby?* South Melbourne. Macmillan.
Yashima, T. (1955), *Crow Boy*. New York. Viking.

Index